D1520189

Heroic Habits

HEROIC HABITS

Discovering the Soul's Potential for Greatness

Fr. Ezra Sullivan, OP

TAN Books
Gastonia, North Carolina

Nihil obstat
  Basil Cole, OP
  Censor deputatus

Imprimi potest
  Ken Letoile, OP
  Prior Provincial, Dominican Province of St. Joseph

The nihil obstat and imprimatur are official declarations that a book or pamphlet is free of doctrinal or moral error. There is no implication that those who have granted the nihil obstat and the imprimi potest agree with the content, opinions or statements expressed therein.

Unless otherwise noted, Scripture quotations are from the Revised Standard Version of the Bible—Second Catholic Edition (Ignatius Edition), copyright © 2006 National Council of the Churches of Christ in the United States of America. Used by permission. All rights reserved.

Cover design by Caroline K. Green

Cover image: The last judgment: detail of the Saints in Paradise, (tempera on wood, 1432-1435), Angelico, Fra (Guido di Pietro/Giovanni da Fiesole) (c.1387-1455) / Italian, Luisa Ricciarini / Bridgeman Images

Library of Congress Control Number: 2021937283

ISBN: 978-1-5051-1747-9
Kindle ISBN: 978-1-5051-1748-6
ePUB ISBN: 978-1-5051-1749-3

Published in the United States by
TAN Books
PO Box 269
Gastonia, NC 28053
www.TANBooks.com

Printed in the United States of America

To the Blessed Virgin Mary,
Mater Misericordiae

CONTENTS

Figures and Tables

ACKNOWLEDGMENTS

With sincere gratitude, I would like to thank the many people who helped this book come about: Fr. Ken Letoile, OP, Prior Provincial of the Province of St. Joseph; Fr. Glenn Morris, OP, Prior of the Convent of Saints Dominic and Sixtus in Rome (the Angelicum community); Fr. Basil Cole, OP, a good friend and the censor for this work; John Murdock, an unfailing friend and brother-in-arms; Michael Sullivan, my biological brother and dear friend, who read every word of this book and gave sage advice (when are your books coming out?); the Dell'Aira, Sheaf, and Umberg families, for their friendship and support; many other religious brothers and sisters, and family and friends, not least the Carmelite Monastery in Georgetown, California. A special word goes to John Moorehouse (+2020), who called me out of the blue to solicit a book for TAN Books, and to Brian Kennelly and the staff at TAN Books, whose hard work helped realize Moorehouse's dream.

CHAPTER 1

A SAINT'S HABITS

He hurriedly dipped his quill in the ink-pot, trying to remember the last words that echoed in his ears. Almost without thinking, the scribe allowed the wisdom to flow from his hand onto the yellow vellum. In a glance, he assessed his progress: his writing trailed more than half-way down the animal skin that had been scraped and stretched and now bore the marks of a miniscule script. He took a breath and blocked out the sound of the three other scribes scribbling away; he forced himself not to consider what the speaker was saying to the fellow next to him. Instead, he focused on what he had to write: "Therefore, there can be such a disturbance of anger that the tongue is entirely impeded from the use of speech. The result is being tight-lipped."

"I'm almost there myself," the scribe thought.

He had been sitting on the unpadded bench in the unheated room for three hours. The skin on his knuckles was cracking from the dry cold, and his foot felt itchy. His stomach growled: it was a fasting day. With his peripheral vision, he could see the speaker, dressed in white, overflowing with buoyant energy and sober passion.

"Doesn't he ever get tired? Isn't he hungry? The sacristan told me he was up all night praying. He's probably forgotten to eat again. God, come to my assistance!"

From his wandering thoughts, the friar brought his attention back to the page. Just as he was finishing up a paragraph, the speaker approached the scribe's desk.

"Brother Reginald, mark a new section. Prologue. Now that we have considered human acts and passions, we will now consider the principles of human acts. The first of these is the intrinsic principle of human acts—namely, habits."

Making small marks on the parchment, Reginald replied, "Yes, Brother." He took another breath, flexed his fingers, and felt his heart lighten from being closer to his friend. Then he plunged back into the text that would become known as the *Summa Theologiae* of his fellow Dominican, Thomas Aquinas.

***

Aquinas's impact on the world can hardly be calculated. His contemporary Bernard Gui would write, "The teaching of Thomas has become an object of admiration for almost the entire world. It instructs the studious, corrects the wayward, guides the wanderer. For he teaches divine matters in the way which most aptly and discreetly employs all those human means which can serve in the work of men's salvation." Gui argued that the brilliance and subtlety of Aquinas's intellect was manifest in "his vast literary output, his many original discoveries, his deep understanding of Scriptures."

At the height of his powers, Aquinas was phenomenally prolific. In terms of a sheet of today's printer paper, Aquinas was writing an average of nearly twelve and a half pages of words a day, every day, all year long. Many scholars would be content if even one of their books were read by specialists in a hundred years. By the end of his short life—less than fifty years—Thomas Aquinas had composed a series of lengthy treatises that are still considered among the most important and profound works of theology and philosophy ever written. Nearly eight hundred years later, they remain influential around the world to specialists and amateurs alike.

What was the secret of Thomas's productivity?

We can quickly dismiss the idea that he wrote so much simply because he had secretaries at his disposal. Assistants may have multiplied Aquinas's strength, but it was *his strength*. According to Gui, "His memory was extremely rich and retentive: whatever he had once read and grasped he never forgot; it was as if knowledge were ever increasing in his soul as page is added to page in the writing of a book." In Thomas's language, he was the "primary" human cause of the text, and the scribes were collaborative "secondary" causes. Thousands of pages, tens of thousands of objections and replies, and millions of words were written because there was something in Thomas Aquinas that gave him the power to harness his mnemonic energy, as well as that of his secretaries, to produce an astounding result.

What was in him?

We have already seen his answer: habits. For Aquinas, a good habit was not a mere repeated pattern of behavior but also the principle underlying them. A habit is the coiled spring of interior strength, the source of personal flourishing, the "intrinsic principle of human acts."

Aquinas was able to do what he did because of his habits. More than that, he was able to *be who he was* because of his habits. "A minimum of time allowed to sleeping and eating," Gui notes, "and all the rest given to prayer or reading or thinking or writing or dictating." While every great person has at least some great habits, Aquinas went a step further than nearly all of them. He unlocked the secret of habits. In addition to developing and exercising his habits to an extraordinary degree, he gave us his own insights about how we might achieve greatness in our own way—and he did so above all in his *Treatise on Habits*.

Aquinas's *Treatise on Habits* in his *Summa Theologiae* is one of his greatest and most unique contributions to Catholic ethics. No other great Catholic writer has a treatise on habits—not Augustine, nor John Chrysostom, nor Bonaventure; not Scotus, nor Robert Bellarmine, nor Alphonsus Liguori; no Church Father, no medieval scholastic, no modern mold-breaker. Despite this fact, Aquinas's rich exposition on the nature and growth of habits has been neglected through the centuries. Thomist moral theologians and ethicists have preferred to mine his thought on flashy ideas like sin, or complex puzzles like human action, or issues able to be politically weaponized like natural law. A handful of references in scholarly works point to Aquinas's insights on habits, but they have been little more than trail markers hinting at more to come. Until now.

Why This Book Is Different

Upon looking at this book, some readers might think, "Another book on habits? There are so many out there. They've sold millions of copies, helped so many people. How can this book make a difference in a crowded market?"

In response, I would point out that the best books on habits ought to contain three key elements: science, practice, and theory.

Representing a *scientific* approach, William James in the nineteenth century helped psychologists and scientists investigate human habits on a formal and empirical level. The advent of neuroscientific techniques and biological chemistry have more recently enabled researchers to develop models of the effects habits have on the brain and nervous system. Nevertheless, contemporary scientific works that address habits are necessarily narrow, as the following illustration indicates.

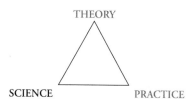

Although their research generates a lot of data and they have good scientific technique, there is often a lack of integrative insight and practical applicability. If you are lucky, you can find practical tips either in the last few sentences of an equation-laden article or baked into a heavy textbook that specialists lug around.

In contrast, texts that focus on *habit-practice* have the advantage of being more accessible. Written for the average reader, these popular books provide practical and entertaining accounts of habit acquisition and development, as the following illustration indicates.

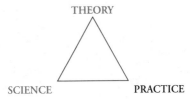

The best popular habit literature incorporates science, at least indirectly. But even when they are not oversimplifying complexity, practically none of them are based on a rich understanding of the human person. Their theory is typically as thin as that of the average disposable self-help book.

Then there are books that cover *habit-theory* in a deep and systematic way. These works are rare, and most of them are in Latin commentaries on Aquinas's own work. Their language, complexity, antiquity, and lack of practical advice leaves them moldering on dusty bookshelves.

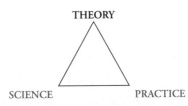

The few English-language books that have attempted to make Aquinas's theory accessible and practical have narrowed in on specific applications such as health or addiction.

Finally, there is the book you are reading right now. It draws upon the best of the science, practice, and theory on habits. The synthesis is possible because it is undergirded by the theology and philosophy of Thomas Aquinas. There is no other book like it.

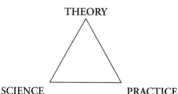

The present book is founded on my extensive research, some of which was published in *Habits and Holiness: Ethics, Theology, and Biopsychology* (Catholic University of America Press, 2021). That book contains more practical tips, but it also wades through many scientific and scholarly debates that will not detain us here. The two books complement and supplement each other. Neither can fully replace the other. To be the most helpful, I offer the most practical advice in this book up front, in chapter 2. That way, as you read later chapters, you can implement what you learned earlier.

A "bonus feature" of this book is that it draws extensively from the lives of the saints. This is no Catholic quirk. Practical books need stories to illustrate and exemplify the lessons therein. The nature of a thing is most apparent when it is in optimal form, and the saints are those who have reached an optimal human condition because of their habits. They lived out their habits heroically.

Although extraordinary people have developed Olympian habits in one area or another, few have had great habits in all of the most important areas. Tiger Woods may have been a Mozart at golf, but he was less than a Yoko Ono at marital fidelity. In contrast, the great saints were heroic in all their

moral habits as a whole. Their skill-sets were radically diversified. Some, like Aquinas, were superhumanly productive
in their works, whereas others were more contemplative and
manifested less exterior productivity. But all the saints were
heroic *spiritually*, for heroism in one great habit entails heroism in all habits that count the most.

Hence, the lives and reflections of the saints are best suited
to help guide us along the way to developing our best habits
to the highest degree. As Aquinas states in his commentary
on the book of Job, "God not only orders the lives of the just
for their own good but also renders them visible for others"
so that we might profit from their example.

Why This Book Will Help You

There is something true to the claim that the Angelic Doctor's work is hard and dry. But it is true for reasons similar to
why a lobster is hard and dry: its skeleton is on the outside.
Many scholars of Aquinas take it to be their job to host a
"Thomistic lobster bake": to trap one of those decapods and
serve up the meaty bits with butter. With that metaphor
in mind, one might suppose that my role in this book is to
copy down faithfully the thought of Aquinas on habit and
to add my own commentary and examples to make Thomas
tastier for the palate.

That's not the way I see it.

If developing habits were as easy as eating buttery food,
then we all would be heroes merely by reading self-help
books.

But that is not the case. All personal habits come at a personal cost. The ones you acquire are at the cost of your disciplined efforts, and even the habits given by God cost your cooperation with his grace. Simply scanning the words of the page can at best develop your knowledge and *dispose* you for developing habits in other realms of your life. Even then, you are doing the scribe's share of the work. Indeed, to benefit from a book on habits, *you* must be a Brother Reginald and your soul must be the vellum on which you write the lessons you learn from Aquinas and the other masters you will meet. If up to now you feel that your life has been less of an epic and more of a farce, do not worry: the point of this book is to help you gain those heroic habits that will truly make your story one worth retelling.

While this work is rooted in Thomas's ideas and develops them in light of the best science and practical insights that are now available, it is not a mere repetition of his insights. It will not only guide you to develop better atom-sized habits that are of immediate practical benefit but also help you establish the right goals for your life, giving you a deep sense of clarity and conviction for the long road ahead. It will also help you receive God-sized habits that only the divine author can write within you.

Your nature is like parchment. You have been stretched and scraped through experience, much like vellum in preparation for writing. Through your conscious actions, you have written and doodled on your soul. Some script has faded away and is difficult to read; other paragraphs you have underlined; others you have crossed out; some stories you have tried to re-write; still others you have written over and over again. God is an author as well. Not only did he give you the vellum but when you invite him, he writes on your soul. Then there is the devil, who tries to interfere and blot out what God has written, or to obscure it with graffiti. The work of acquiring habits is similar to grasping a quill in your hand and writing the story of your character, the tale you are telling about yourself.

The work of cooperating with God's way of writing habits into your soul is similar to the way the writers of Sacred Scripture cooperated with divine inspiration. In Aquinas's view, there were two authors of Scripture: "one divine and principal, the other human and instrumental." The principal agent makes his contribution through the instrumentality of the secondary agent. Through the shape of the quill's nib, an author makes his mark on the page; through a human's thoughts, feelings, and very life, the divine author writes the story of a saint-in-the-making. This is what Thomas's biographers meant when they said he was an "admirable instrument of the Holy Spirit." God used the friar's own humanity to create something extraordinary. The first extraordinary thing was Thomas himself; and secondly, man of his exterior works were extraordinary, even heroic. It follows that Aquinas's profound theory of habits, incarnated in his own life, will ultimately make this book on habits more practical. Better theory leads to more effective practice. It is my hope that this book can help you cooperate with the Holy Spirit so that, with God, you may write onto the parchment of your soul many heroic habits.

What to Expect

The typical self-help book is full of wooden formulae about how to live a happier life. Some even propose algorithms to live by as strategies for better human living. Catholics often follow suit—unfortunately. Whether justified or not, traditional Catholic morality has the reputation of being a series of legalisms and rule-sets. Many authors have reinforced that perspective to the point of insisting that the chief way to holiness is to have a "rule of life" and innumerable little rules that govern every year, month, week, day, and even every minute of our lives. That is not the approach of Thomas Aquinas, and it is not the approach of this book.

Law has two primary purposes: to impel us to do something good and to restrain us from doing something evil. Exterior rules of life are necessary to give us a push when we are not inclined to do good and to hold us back when we are inclined to do evil. They provide guidelines if we do not know what to do in the moment, or when we waver in the face of temptation. In this way, rules can be like parents who nudge their children to act politely, to excel in school, to eat healthy food, and to pray before bedtime. All of these are good behaviors. If the rules are never internalized, though, if the person never comes to maturely grasp the import of the rules and make their spirit his own, he can slowly become infantilized. He could allow someone else to make the rules of life for him while his brain goes on auto-pilot, or he could follow a rule in some exterior manner without the more difficult and important work of transforming his interior life.

Eventually, a person comes to see that hyper-specific exterior rules of life can never account for the roadblocks and blind turns that he encounters along the road. "Lift up your heart to God every sixty seconds." That's a great rule. But it requires exceptions: "Lift up your heart to God every sixty seconds *unless doing so distracts you from other duties that require all of your attention, such as brain surgery or NASCAR driving.*" The rule is thus transformed: "Lift up your heart to God every sixty seconds *when reasonable.*" That last part, the "reasonable" portion, is where the habit of prudence comes into play. Prudence is the habit of mental maturity whereby we know the right thing to do, and our intellect commands us to do it in the right way, at the right time. We are not autonomous driving vehicles. Instead of being guided solely by an exterior law, we must interiorize it through prudently-guided habits.

Bad motives may also corrupt a legalistic way of life. It is all too easy to follow a rule from a base fear of being punished, or from craving the rewards of obedience, as a child might ace all his tests to avoid punishment for bad marks or to receive money. Unfortunately, legalism leads people to think they are developing themselves merely by adhering to some behavioral norms for achievement. Human flourishing means more. Flourishing requires the full use of the mind; it also requires the broad development of the heart. Thomas insists that only two "rules of life" are absolutely necessary for our perfection: love of God and love of neighbor. As St. Paul said, "Love is the fulfilling of the law" (Rm 13:10).

Do not mistake me for an antinomian. My approach does not ignore the real value imparted by good law. Indeed, I think one of the chief vices in our day is the rejection of God's law, the moral law, the natural law. My point is that just as no series of rules can make a scribbler into a great writer, so no rule of life is sufficient for developing heroic habits. Rules do help. Principles, in the sense of flexible guidelines, help even more. I will offer some along the way. My primary aim, however, is not to help you change your exterior behavior by force of wooden rules. Rather, it is to help you change your *interior life* with the grace of God—that is, through developing acquired and infused habits. Once that happens—and it may take a long time and a lot of suffering—you will find that doing the right thing comes more easily, quickly, sweetly, and skillfully. Your habits will have become heroic.

CHAPTER 2

HABIT MODELS

In the 1991 movie *What About Bob?* Bill Murray plays Bob, an innocent psychiatric patient who has difficulty getting by in life. He eventually finds success by following the advice to take "baby steps" to accomplish his bigger goals. Bob engages in imaginative self-talk: "Baby steps out the hall; baby steps onto the elevator. . . . One little step at a time, and I can do anything!" Bob's little victories illustrate how difficult things ought to be reached by way of easy ones.

Human behavior is notoriously difficult to comprehend. You are the most complex creature in existence. As a human, you are an organic and harmonious body-soul union. Your soul makes you as potentially unfathomable as angels, and your body makes you more complicated than a quantum supercomputer. To understand human action and habituation is no simple task. Fortunately, there are proven shortcuts. A letter attributed to Aquinas on "How to Study" recommends that we should choose to enter the ocean not straightaway but instead by the little streams. This hints at the value of modeling reality.

Models of the cosmos populate the palaces of our minds. We walk in a world of symbols, and our brains naturally register the models around us similar to how soft wax easily receives impressions from a mold. For example, pre-speech infants are able to somehow grasp that simple shapes like triangles and squares can represent human-like behavior. While watching a carefully designed cartoon, a group of babies preferred triangles and circles that interacted cooperatively, and they rejected a square that acted violently toward the other shapes.

As people develop, they gradually make and use models of the world in increasingly sophisticated ways. Young children play with figurines to act out friendships and family dynamics. Elementary school children draw maps of fictional worlds. Architects draw blueprints; sculptors carve miniatures; city planners fashion scaled-down neighborhoods; and mathematicians and scientists develop and explain models of the bones and marrow of the universe. Those who want to more quickly and easily develop heroic habits use models of human behavior.

A model is a symbolic representation of a small set of ideas that abstracts from less relevant details. Models are enormously useful. They help us to better understand and interact with a complex reality by offering us a simpler, more tractable version of it. By cutting away extraneous information, models also act like scalpels and uncover the bare bones of definitions and assumptions.

In this chapter, I present two distinct models that serve as analogies for human actions and habits: one from contemporary thought, the other from Aquinas. Then I propose a model that unites them together and utilizes their respective strengths. My multi-model approach offers "baby steps" that help habituate us to think clearly about habits. I begin by analyzing the habit loop model because it will be familiar to many readers.

Circular Thinking: Habits and Loops

Talk of a "trigger warning" is fairly frequent nowadays, but few know that it is rooted in habit studies conducted by behaviorist psychologists. Ivan Pavlov, of rinstance, showed that a dog could be "triggered" by the sound of a bell to salivate even in the absence of food. A stimulus or antecedent to a habituated behavior can thus be called a trigger: once activated, it sets into motion a definite activity similar to how the trigger of a gun initiates a bullet's flight. Later researchers, such as E. L. Thorndike and B. F. Skinner, more thoroughly explained how environment, rewards, and punishments affect habits. They laid the foundations for the habit loop model, which suggests that there are three basic elements to behavior. It's as easy as A-B-C.

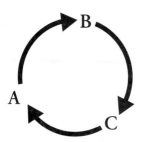

- *Antecedent* or stimulus which initiates a behavior. Colloquially called a "trigger."
- *Behavior*, an external and observable movement of an animal that has been "triggered."
- *Consequent*, the result of the behavior.

Antecedent/trigger A tends to initiate behavior B. When a positive consequent C follows, it constitutes a reward that reinforces the power of antecedent A to produce behavior B, thus creating a loop of behavior. When the loop runs its course enough times, it creates an inclination to perform a habitual behavior, and a habit loop comes into existence.

Habit is a stable inclination, a quality of the soul, that impels us to respond to some stimulus in a regular way. One of the chief powers of a habit is the quasi-automatic behavioral patterns that it induces. Habitual responses can be useful in themselves when they aid the accomplishment of some good. Habits often help people to focus their attention and energy in a laser-like fashion on some action, such as writing, by freeing their minds from the distraction of a simultaneous supportive task, such as thinking about dinner. Habits can exist on a number of different levels, depending on what part of ourselves has become habituated. Consider the following examples ordered from less conscious to more conscious habituation—a similar pattern works through them.

Learning to walk. Although walking is practically natural to all humans, an infant must be habituated to do so. Once the motor-skill habit has been fully inculcated, a person will retain that habit for the rest of her life. Being able to walk frees you up for all sorts of other simultaneous tasks, such as navigating with a map or talking with a friend.

Learning to write. Although children can pick up the basics of a spoken language with little conscious practice, writing is a skill that requires the cooperation of a child who learns it. Some children need stronger rewards or punishments to develop the stable disposition to form letters on a page, to string words together, and to string sentences together correctly. Once the skill is fully engrained, a person is then freer to communicate more effectively.

Driving a car. The mechanical skill of driving requires conscious choice on the part of the driver, typically a person entering maturity. The task of driving, when combined with skills related to navigation, can absorb nearly all of the concentration of a new driver. However, as the skills are mastered, and the habit becomes second nature, you can operate a car almost automatically—as every commuter knows.

Ethical actions. Although not a mechanical skill like the others in this list, many elements of ethical actions can become habituated, such that doing the right thing comes from a deeply-embedded impulse of the will. A doctor might learn the principles of medical ethics and practice them so consistently that he no longer needs to ask himself what to do in an emergency. A mother might love her children so strongly that she almost automatically cares for them when they are injured. A believer hardly needs to think about the words and actions in Mass and can focus more on interior prayer while actively participating.

These various examples show that because habituation entails possessing a stable disposition that enables certain automatic processes, when a habit is deliberately inculcated or developed, its use in adults is voluntary. Good habits perfect and direct one's natural powers and thereby help a person to achieve more than he could have without the habit. Consequently, Aquinas argues that we can act in *a fully human way* only by employing good habits.

Habit Loops and Habit Change

Now that we have seen the basic structure of habits, we can consider how to use them to our advantage. To develop or change a habit, you can focus on one or all of the elements of a habit loop.

- *Antecedent*: You can focus on triggers—events, places, times, etc.—and either avoid the triggers that lead to unwanted behaviors or choose triggers that lead to wanted behaviors.
- *Behavior*: You can change behaviors by practicing desired acts or by substituting desired acts in place of undesired behaviors.
- *Consequent*: You can change the effects that follow from your behavior. To reinforce desired acts, you can increase or intensify positive results; to avoid reinforcing undesired behaviors, you can increase negative results (punishments) or decrease positive results from the undesired behavior.

A simple example can illustrate the power of antecedents/triggers to develop habits. It is said that St. Benedict wanted to be more faithful to Christ's injunction to "always pray and not lose heart" (Lk 18:1). How to do it? The master of monks decided that whenever he walked through an archway, he would lift up his mind to God. The enormous abbey Monte Cassino, with its great doors and colonnades, must have afforded many opportunities for prayer as St. Benedict passed through it on his way to prayer and work. Put schematically:

- *Antecedent*: archway
- *Behavior*: short prayer
- *Consequent*: greater union with God

The habit loop came in handy once when a man asked me to help him stop yelling so often at his wife and children. I asked him to explain what antecedents set off his bad behavior: A bad day at work? A messy house? Disobedient children? After a thoughtful pause, he said that as soon as he set one foot in the door after work, his wife bombarded him with complaints, information about house repairs, random thoughts, demands to discipline the children, and so on. Simultaneously, his four kids would be running around, shouting and whining, asking for help with their homework, accusing each other of naughtiness, begging for a cookie. "Every day when I come home from the stresses of the office, it feels like I'm storming the shores of Normandy after having swum the English Channel," he said. "Now I know why some guys go to the bar first."

We agreed that he needed a new habit. Studies indicate that plans to negate a habituated trigger-response—telling oneself, "When my family clamors for attention, I will *not* be angry"—often fail. Instead, such avoidance plans either reinforce the association between the trigger and the behavior or make a person *more* attentive and sensitive to such triggers. Furthermore, trying to endure the situation quietly without changing anything would be almost impossible given that he was in the habit of cathartic yelling.

I suggested that he learn how to avoid being triggered by their behavior. "Going to the bar will create other bad habits. But calming down before you enter your home may help. I recommend sitting in your car for a few minutes every day before you come home. Rest, think about the day, say a prayer to God for your work and family. Then transition from one space to the other mentally and spiritually before you walk through the door."

Later on, the harried husband and father reported positive results. He said he started to look forward to his little daily prayer time in the car. This new practice strengthened him to address the concerns of his wife and children more rationally.

Antecedent	demanding family
Behavior	yelling dad
Consequent	everyone less happy

replaced with:

Antecedent	prayer in car
Behavior	calm and cheerful dad amid demanding family
Consequent	everyone happier

When behavior patterns are more complex, it may help to use the habit loop more methodically. To illustrate, I am going to walk through the example of Frank and his undesired behavior of overeating. Although based on a real person, the presentation is more formal to highlight the distinct elements of the habit loop model.

In order to eliminate overeating, Frank analyzed his behavior in light of the A-B-Cs of the habit loop. After some self-observation, he started to notice the following:

- *Behavior*. Humongous meals were not Frank's problem. Like his Italian friends, his breakfast consisted of an espresso and a pastry—or, if he was especially hungry, an espresso, a pastry, and a cigarette. His lunch and dinner were usually moderate. But Frank would munch throughout the night.
- *Antecedent*. What triggered his snacking? It didn't seem as if it were mere hunger or the time of day. Frank noticed that typically he would reach for the artery-clogging nibbles while reclining on the couch and watching TV. He decided that "watching TV" was the main trigger for his binge eating.
- *Consequent*. The beer and salty snacks felt so rewarding that Frank started to look forward to watching TV just so he could have them.

Frank had a few options for addressing his behavior of overeating.

- *Antecedent. One way to eliminate a habitual behavior is to avoid what triggers it.* Frank was unwilling to give up evening entertainment, so this option was a non-starter for him.
- *Consequent. Another way to eliminate a habitual*

behavior is to substitute one reward for another. Contentment from eating seemed to be the desired reward, so Frank tried eating healthier snacks. But a belly of plain carrots did not satisfy, so he started dousing them in ranch sauce. The topping only intensified his craving for the munchies he really liked. After five days, he returned to the potato chips and Budweiser.

- *Behavior.* *To make a habitual behavior more acceptable, one can alter the most problematic aspect of the behavior.* Unconvinced that he had enough will power to stop eating his fattening foods, Frank decided that he would try to change his behavior. To counter overeating, Frank tried to count his calories throughout the day. By eating a smaller lunch and dinner, he could have "spare" calories in the evening that he could then "spend" on his snacks. At first, this technique helped Frank reduce his overall caloric intake. But Frank never had the motivation to measure his food precisely, or to control his eating. Soon he gave up the technique and took up binging even more, while asking himself, "Why am I doing this to myself? Where is my life going, anyway? What's the point?"

Some behaviorist psychologists would argue that deep questions are inconsequential to getting results. They could even hinder results by distracting a person from more effective ways to measure and control one's behavior. Legalistic advice would argue for more precise rules and more fidelity to the rules. Pragmatic advice would tell Frank to knuckle down and use a better technique. If a new technique does not work, keep experimenting until you see results. Both approaches might help, but there is more to the story.

Frank's anguished bewilderment at his failure shows that soul-searching never ceases for a person who desires real change. Exclusive focus on exterior things leads to a circular thinking that cannot provide answers outside of measurable, empirical reality. If a person desires the greatest change, he will either look into himself or he will stop searching for the truth. As Mortimer Adler would say, we are all philosophers wanting to ask the deepest questions. In the unforgettable phrase of Aristotle, "all men by nature desire to know." Sometimes we set aside profound questions for the sake of the simpler questions of practicality, but what is in the depths will eventually surface like air bubbles in water. This leads us to Aquinas's model of human behavior.

Linear Thinking: Actions and Arrows

Wisdom was Aquinas's goal in sharing his thought. He beautifully states, "Among all human pursuits, the pursuit of wisdom is more perfect, more sublime, more useful, and more joyful." The highest sort of wisdom, the Dominican noted, seeks to explain things in terms of their highest causes. In considering habits, therefore, Aquinas is concerned less about events and techniques that change behavior and more about the nature of habits and human action itself, especially their origins in the depths of a person's soul. Since the core techniques of the habit loop were developed through experiments on dogs, mice, and chickens, the model remains unmoored from a robust account of intention and meaning in habits. It is precisely here that Aquinas can help.

To hit the mark and center in on the nature of habits, we would do well to see the arrow as a model for properly human action. St. Thomas Aquinas often uses the arrow as a model to explain action. According to Aquinas, there are two basic categories of human behavior: a properly human action and a mere action of a human.

First, there is a properly "human action," whereby a person moves himself toward some foreseen end by making a deliberate decision. This is analogous to an archer deliberately shooting an arrow, an act that imparts directed motion or intentionality to the arrow. All human actions—such as deliberately singing, working, reading, or praying—have this arrow-like directed motion. Shakespeare echoed this insight, writing:

> As many arrows, loosed several ways,
> Come to one mark; as many ways meet in one town;
> As many fresh streams meet in one salt sea; . . .
> So may a thousand actions, once afoot,
> End in one purpose.

Note that, in the Bard's description, arrows and properly human actions are "loosed" and "afoot"; that is, they have a dynamism and movement coming from a person's choice. Additionally, a huge number of arrows and actions can fly toward "one mark" and "one purpose"; that is, they have a shared directionality and goal.

The second kind of behavior is a mere "action of a human," which is not activated by immediate choice. This is analogous to some indeliberate behavior of the archer toward the arrow, like accidentally dropping one out of a quiver. In contrast to a properly human act, which derives from the intellect and will coordinately producing a deliberate choice, a mere act of a human arises from non-deliberative sources, such as reflexes, emotions, or the imagination. An action of a human is therefore a less-than-intentional behavior, like absent-mindedly scratching oneself, being startled at a loud noise, or licking one's lips when seeing a tasty dessert.

The two basic categories of human behavior give rise to two basic kinds of habits. Repeated human actions develop human habits, whereas repeated non-deliberate behaviors give rise to mere non-deliberate habits. The difference between the two is vast. Suppose a person consciously cultivates kindness toward her new coworkers while she simultaneously but unknowingly adopts their taste for black tea. Kindness is a moral good, whereas food preferences are morally neutral. Although these two kinds of habits develop alongside each other, they are fundamentally different in origin and meaning.

Aquinas's basic view of human action and habits can be described as linear because he focuses on the goal of an action. For him, the two chief elements of human action—and a habit that develops from it—are the action itself and its chosen end. A tertiary element to human action is what Aquinas calls "circumstance," which is whatever stands aside from the object and the chosen goal of the agent. Taken together, these three elements provide a model of human action comparable to an arrow in flight.

- *Object: what you do*. What an archer does is shoot an arrow. The objective act which an archer performs is shooting—namely, releasing a pointed projectile called an arrow from a string in order to put it into flight. To put it another way, the proper object of an archer's act is shooting an arrow. Likewise, every acting person performs some particular action that possesses its own behavioral intelligibility or "object." The object of an act is the intrinsic point to the action itself. Because human action by its nature is not random or accidental, one can know what a person is doing by analyzing the objective nature of the act, which exists regardless of the agent's subjective feeling about it or his further intention for it. For example, when a person releases an arrow from a bow string, he is objectively shooting the arrow, even if he does so regretfully or in order to accomplish some other end by means of his shot, such as shaming the sheriff of Nottingham.

  Note that the object of an action defines what the action *is*. To recognize the object is to know what sort of action is being performed, which can only be discovered through a careful consideration of the exterior behavior as well as the acting person's intention. Aquinas's philosophical theology is crucial in this regard. Contrastingly, a more behaviorist approach does not define an action so much as account for its measurable aspects: how often one performs it, under what conditions, etc.

- *End: why you do it*. When an archer aims an arrow at a target, the arrow in flight gains that target as the purpose of its flight. A spectator might ask, "Why is the arrow flying that direction?" The archer answers, "To hit that target." "Why do you want to hit the target?" another asks. "To win the prize," the archer replies. When a person aims his action at a chosen goal, also called a purpose or an end, his action takes on some of the quality of that intended end. The end of an action is that for which a person performs the act, also called his intention. "Why am I overeating?" one might ask himself. The answer could be "to feel better" or "to make Grandma happy." That for the sake of which one performs the act can be known by considering one's intentions, whether hidden or manifest.

- *Circumstances: what affects your action*. Circumstances for the act of shooting the arrow illustrate circumstances for any other act: they include the height and weight of the archer, wind conditions, the color of the target, acts that immediately preceded the shooting, the effects of shooting the arrow, and many other things that are aside from the substance of the act and its end. Note that, for Aquinas, the antecedent trigger represents only one of many circumstances of an act. The effect of an act, which includes its potential rewarding character, constitutes another circumstance. For

Aquinas, the most important circumstances are those that affect the agent's intention in performing the act.

Repeatedly performing an action will tend to produce a habit to repeat that action. Overeating regularly inclines you to overeat again. Modern parlance typically refers to a habit as a *repeated act*, such as overeating regularly, whereas Aquinas denotes a habit as the itching *inclination* which urges a person to perform a repeated act. In his view, a habit cannot be reduced to an external event; it is primarily the latent but dynamic interior inclination to repeat an act. When a person says "I have a habit of overeating," they mean that they not only frequently overeat but also possess an *urging tendency* to do so. Repeatedly performing some act produces inclinations to perform similar acts in the future. Accordingly, Aquinas defines a habit as an acquired and stable inclination that tends to reproduce similar acts, with a relation to the object of the habit and its end.

To understand a habit you possess, you can analyze it in terms of the object, end, and circumstance of its proper act. Suppose that you have the habit of overeating. You might consider the following.

- *What was I doing?* (Object) Overeating. Giving a precise measurement for how much you eat relates more to behaviorist concerns, whereas defining what counts as "too much" is more of Aquinas's concern, as it concerns the natural purposes of eating. Clearly, the two ways of looking at an action can complement each other. When you accurately evaluate that you ate more than was good for your overall health, then you know that you ate too much.

- *Why did I do it?* (End) To relieve loneliness? To increase energy in order to continue working despite lethargy? The goal toward which one directs a habitual behavior tells you about the nature of the habit within the soul.

- *What significantly affected my action?* (Circumstances) Relevant circumstances are those that significantly affected your action. If a feeling of sadness and the tastiness of the dish inclined you to eat more, then mood and quality of food were relevant circumstances.

Sometimes focusing on just one of these elements can initiate meaningful change in our lives.

Objective behavior. Suppose that a person is dissatisfied with living in a certain condition but is unsure of why that condition exists. In that case, a person should start with an objective analysis of the situation and ask "What am I doing?" Patricia knew that she was overweight but thought her condition might be caused by genetics, since her parents and sisters were also obese. To test her theory, Patricia kept a food diary. To her surprise, she discovered that she was eating four full meals a day, plus snacks, plus sugary drinks. Knowledge of her own behavior helped her realize that genetics were probably not the only cause: she was eating more than nourishment required. This self-knowledge helped her set goals for more moderate eating.

End and *Circumstances* (Example 1). In the previous section on the habit loop, we saw that Frank knew that he overate, but he didn't know precisely why. It took a good deal of honest and painful soul-searching to discover his deeper motivations. While overeating, Frank had not articulated to himself that his goal was to ease his sadness. But he knew that he was single and without many friends, and fatty and sugary foods gave him a temporary feeling of fullness and satisfaction. The pleasure of the food slightly eased the ache of an empty apartment. With insight into his intentions, Frank saw that although he could not immediately or easily relieve his loneliness, he should try to avoid eating comfort foods as a substitute for companionship.

End and *Circumstances* (Example 2). In contrast to Frank, Bobby was married. His wife suggested that he was eating candy during work because he was not getting enough rest at night. The lack of sleep lowered his vigor and focus throughout the day, which he tried to overcome with a sugar-fueled boost. Consequently, Bobby focused on fixing his sleep patterns rather than worrying about some deeper psychological meaning to his snacking.

Notice that the relation between end and circumstances were different for Frank and Bobby. Frank's singleness was an extremely relevant circumstance because being alone inclined him to feel lonely, which then inclined him to overeat for comfort. In contrast, Bobby's marital status seemed to be fairly irrelevant to his overeating since his goal in snacking was to increase flagging energy while at work. Objectively, they were both overeating, but the further purpose for which they overate was radically different. Consequently, their habits were radically different: Frank's habit was ultimately directed toward comforting himself in the midst of loneliness, whereas Bobby's habit was directed toward being a more effective worker. One tended toward the vice of intemperance, whereas the other tended toward the virtue of industriousness. Thus we can see the importance of considering a habit in terms of the object of the act from whence it springs, as well as the further end of the person who directs his habitual actions.

The Best of Both Models

Up to this point, I have described the habit loop and the linear model of habituation. Both are valuable, but they are distinct. Here I would like to discuss the advantages and disadvantages of both and then show how they might be combined in order to supplement each other.

One advantage of the habit loop is its demonstrable efficacy. Studies have shown that utilizing the habit loop properly can help people achieve their goals for self-change between 66 and 84 percent of the time. One reason for the power of this technique is that it requires many precise measurements: what came immediately before an undesired behavior, the extent to which a person performed a behavior, how much time the behavior took, what responses resulted in the person from his behavior. In the habit loop, A leads to B, which leads to C, which re-starts the movement at A again, with no apparent development or goal. This model makes sense for sub-rational animals who do not have personally-chosen goals. A dog's goals are provided by its instincts or its trainer.

To the extent that humans are like sub-rational animals, the model works for us as well. By coming to know these things, a person comes to know more about himself and how he is affected by his environment.

A significant drawback to the habit loop is that it does not explain personal motivations for developing habits, or how habits fit into a person's lifestyle and nature. In other words, it does not explain human action insofar as it is specifically human—that is, as it engages our intellect and volition. Behaviorist psychology and techniques typically do not ask the deeper questions: *Why am I doing this behavior? What does my behavior mean? How does it affect my character? Does it make me a better person?* Thus, the habit loop model does not distinguish between deliberate acts and non-deliberate movements. It cannot, because it lacks a robust explanation of free choice. Consequently, both fall under the umbrella term *behavior*. Intentionality and directedness are confined in a black box. Indeed, the circular shape of the habit loop symbolizes its directionless character. The habit loop model thus has real, verifiable value for helping a person to develop good habits and eliminate bad ones, but it calls for a deeper engagement with what makes us most human. This is precisely where Aquinas's model may help.

The advantages of a Thomistic arrow model for human action include that it targets the soul of habits. By giving an accurate account of how the intellect and will operate to produce a deliberate choice, Aquinas shows that human habits are voluntary and shape our moral life. By discussing how the objects of performed acts develop habits within us, Aquinas helps us to see the objective nature of habits. By emphasizing the importance of intended ends for action, Aquinas shows that a habit's dynamic system has directionality and can be pointed toward beatitude or damnation.

In Aristotelian language, the habit loop focuses on efficient causes of habits to the neglect of formal and final causes, whereas Aquinas's linear model focuses on the formal and final causes of habits. Efficient causes arise first in time, insofar as they initiate motion. The final cause, however, is the most important of the causes, because a thing is said to be perfect insofar as it attains its proper end, which is its ultimate perfection. Furthermore, the final cause, as the good toward which a person tends, impels a person to activate all the other causes to reach it. By focusing on end-directed intentionality, Aquinas's account helps us see the deepest significance of our actions, their consequent habits, and the ultimate direction of our lives.

But disadvantages also accrue to the arrow model. Recognizing in principle that circumstances can alter the moral valence of an act, or even change its species, Aquinas's perspective nevertheless makes it difficult to recognize the importance of circumstances in shaping actions in general. Focusing on the object and end alone make it even more difficult to identify which circumstances are the most important for generating and maintaining a particular act. Finally, because Aquinas is primarily interested in voluntary acts, the arrow model makes little room for explaining and shaping non-deliberate behaviors.

In sum, Aquinas's model tends to be less practical than the behaviorist model. This poses no problem for the theologian; he purposely concentrates his gaze on unchanging heavenly truths rather than at the continually flowing earthly realities at his feet. Consequently, some theologians, with a clumsy use of Aquinas's thought, offer unhelpful advice. A voluntarist spiritual director might encourage a penitent to "try harder" and pray for more "will power" to overcome some temptation—since the primary cause of vice is the will, after all. A more virtue-inclined priest might encourage a penitent to "try to be more just" or "consider the kinds of injustice" in response to a child's confession of not honoring his parents. Without concrete suggestions of *how to do it*, advice in both cases would remain overly abstract. This is precisely where the habit loop model may help because its design enables laser-like focus on what highly specific practices are most likely to produce desired outcomes.

The habit loop and the arrow model are not at odds with each another. Materialist philosophy is inimical to a Catholic understanding of the human person, but the habit loop is not dependent on a reductive viewpoint. Rather, it can be integrated into a Thomistic understanding of action and habits, to the benefit of each. A modified habit loop would look like this.

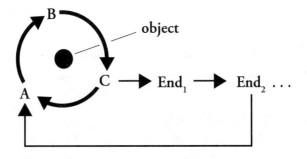

Here we have the familiar habit loop, A-B-C (Antecedent, Behavior, and Consequent), centered around O, the object of the act, and pointed toward the End. Sometimes a person has more than one end in performing a single act; these ends can be ordered to one another. In the example above, Bobby ate extra food so that he might have more energy to work (End$_1$), and he worked in order to support his family (End$_2$). If he wanted to change his behavior, he could decide to temper his food to lose weight (End$_1$); having lower weight would be directed toward feeling healthier and living longer for his family (End$_2$).

The arrow running from End$_2$ toward antecedent A illustrates an important feature of Aquinas's understanding of human action and habits; namely, whatever we intend as an end has a formative effective on how our behavior develops. If a politician intends to feed the poor in order to be praised by others, then the goal of being praised by others—the vanity—shapes the way he goes about giving money: he will smile for the cameras as he ladles soup in his baseball cap and apron. If a person feeds the poor for the love of God, then divine charity will form her generosity: even in the absence of cameras, she will do so with a smile for the poor person.

Aquinas agrees with the observation that a positive reward strengthens a habit. In his vocabulary, *fruition* is the pleasure a person experiences when a person's will rests in the good she sought and achieved. When a gardener cultivates a fruit tree throughout the seasons, and after harvest relishes the taste and feel of a crunchy, sweet Honeycrisp apple, then the likelihood of her cultivating the tree again increases noticeably. Put more formally, an end or goal is some good that a person desires. When a person is united with that good and experiences fruition upon that union, the formative power of the end is increased and her appetite becomes more conformed to that good. Reward, delight in the good achieved, increases the power of an efficient cause—including an antecedent—to induce a similar behavior. She is thereby more inclined to do what it takes to be united with that good in the future. The entire development of a habit can thus be understood as the process by which a person becomes conformed to what is good or what she perceives as good. Now, the desire for good is nothing other than love. Therefore, in some way, all habituation involves the habituation of our love. I will spell out implications of this astounding conclusion in future chapters.

CHAPTER 3

EMOTIONAL HABITS

It was mid-summer in Cincinnati, and I was on a run. The humidity wrapped around my lungs like a damp woolen blanket. "Watch out for the dog near the bend," a Dominican brother had said when I told him my route. As I approached the forewarned spot, I thought, "I don't see any dog. What was he talking about?"

A few paces later, I revised my assessment: "Oh. *That* dog."

It looked like a mix between a Doberman Pinscher and a grizzly bear, but less friendly. I began to hustle. It wasn't chained as it ran parallel to me, howling and slavering to sink its teeth into my leg. I quickly realized that an electronic fence kept the canine on the lawn. Until it didn't. For half a second, the beast paused—then it leaped through the invisible barrier. It let out a yelp as the shock collar did its work. The chase was on. As I picked up my pace, I looked behind and saw its frothy muzzle nearly at my heels. In only a moment, the furry flesh-seeking missile would catch up to me. Right then, an idea jolted into my brain. I took a sharp turn and entered the lawn the dog had just exited. Without slowing down, the pooch, furious to lose it prey, tore after me—and got shocked again. It was dazed this time. I pivoted and left the lawn. We were once again on opposite sides of the invisible fence. The dog stumbled toward me, wary of getting shocked yet again. So I turned on my afterburners and zoomed away. It didn't catch me.

I start my chapter on emotional habits with this story because it can be understood on two levels. On the surface, we notice that both humans and animals have emotions, but questions inevitably arise as we consider them together. Why are some dogs mean and angry but others cuddly and cozy? What makes for fear? Are human emotions basically the same as those of non-humans? On a deeper level, the narrative can be read symbolically. The dog represents our emotions, and the runner represents our reason. What should be done? Should we shun our emotions? Let them have their way with us? According to Aquinas, we can tame our emotions much as a person can tame and train a dog to become his best friend. That is the difficult but rewarding task of habituation.

To provide models for understanding our emotional habits, I will take baby steps along way, beginning with simpler kinds of animals and working my way up to human beings. By meandering through a zoo of creatures and comparing their powers and susceptibility to habituation to ours, we can more easily understand human emotions and how habituation works for us.

Lower Animals and Non-Emotional Habits

All living things, including plants, perform the basic functions of self-maintenance, nutrition, and generation. Within the limits of their bodily structure, they can adapt to new situations in a stable way. The power of habit is so pervasive in the created universe that humans have discovered ways to habituate a huge number of organisms to perform new and useful functions. That is what enables me to "train" the potted English ivy that sits on my windowsill: plant habituation.

Somewhat between flora and fauna are slime molds. Their modest capabilities urge them to move about and develop stable changes, illustrating the basic structure of sensory habituation. Despite lacking a brain, slime molds have the ability to solve mazes and memorize and anticipate periodic environmental changes. They can also be habituated to recognize the harmlessness of salt and coffee and to transfer that information to other slime molds.

Animals manifest greater perfection. All animals are *animate*; that is, they are animated by a substantial and individual life-force that Aquinas recognized as an "animal soul." The soul is the source of self-movement and *sentience*—that is, the power of sensing objects encountered by means of a nervous system—as well as *perception*, which registers sensations, organizes them, estimates the object's potential benefit or harm, and stores the sensations and estimations in memory. These powers enable animals to survive, interact, and reproduce.

Consider the average jellyfish. Gooey, squishy, luminous, and venomous, jellyfish are the most ancient animals in the ocean. The brainless jellyfish possesses a network of neurons that controls their movement and enables habit development. Their unconvoluted nature helps us grasp the essentials of habituation. Experiments have shown that jellyfish can be trained to respond to a stimulus and develop new behaviors of expanding and contracting the central portion of their body, the bell. This change is possible only if jellyfish have, at minimum, the powers of sensation, perception, and movement.

The model below indicates that some antecedent (A) triggers a behavior (B), which consists of three stages. First, the jellyfish senses the stimulus with its sensory powers (S). Second, the sensation is registered by the jelly's perceptive power (P), located in the neural network. Third, the perception activates the motor power (M), which leads to a consequent (C): the jellyfish moves itself. When this series happens many times, as in a loop, the jellyfish becomes habituated to the stimulus.

1. Lower animals

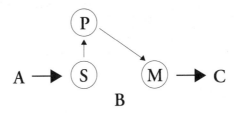

Without pencil or paper, the jellyfish learns. As far back as 1885, George Romanes's research on jellyfish nerve growth explained the physiological foundations of learning, which hold true as much to them as to us. In essence, just as nerve fibers grow in a jellyfish through exercise and effort, so "a child learns its lessons by frequently repeating them; and thus it is that our knowledge is accumulated."

Remarkably, experiments verified these intuitions over a hundred years later. In 2000, Eric Kandel won the Nobel Prize mainly due to his studies of the giant marine snail *Aplysia*. Kandel used habit loop techniques to show that the sea creature's reflexes could be modified by habituation—and this process rewires circuits in its nervous system. Neural rewiring is similar for humans. By repeatedly thinking the same thought, we produce more neurotransmitters and receptors in the brain synapses related to that thought. Brains, like muscles, grow through repeated exercise. The process of developing new brain cells is called neurogenesis, and it can continue even through adulthood. It turns out you can teach an old dog trainer new tricks. But I am anticipating a bit.

Here I would like to focus on the *non-emotional quality* of habituation in lower animals. Bacteria, slime molds, and jellyfish can all be habituated in some basic way. But their behaviors in response to light, heat, salt, and other simple stimuli are undramatic organic processes. Every process of habituation for animals involves movements Aquinas would recognize as analogous to love or hate/disgust. A movement toward what is perceived as helpful to survival could be understood as a rudimentary sort of love. Similarly, a movement away from something perceived as harmful could be categorized as hate or disgust. But these are not emotions in the proper sense: lower creatures simply do not have the neurological equipment for such sophisticated responses to objects in their environment. The jellyfish stings as a matter of cold fact, not from a burst of anger. If a jellyfish develops dispositive habits to swim in a particular way, it still remains carefree, unlike us humans.

Can humans become habituated like the jellyfish in non-emotional, non-deliberate ways? We can, but in a properly human way. Unlike our water-bound squishy-stingy friends, humans have the whole panoply of familiar sensory powers (S): touch, sight, hearing, taste, and smell. We also have more numerous and more developed interior powers of perception (P): the familiar memory and imagination, along with the less familiar powers of estimation and perception-coordination. Compare:

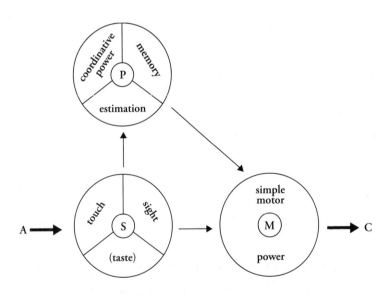

lower animal powers

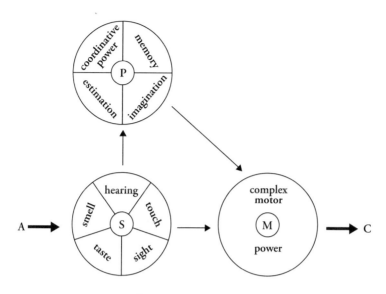

lower powers in a human

Furthermore, even the powers we have in common with lower animals possess a fundamentally different orientation and meaning, because our powers are organically integrated with our entire person, which includes the intellect, and entails loftier goals.

Humans can seemingly develop non-deliberative stable inclinations, since people can perform all sorts of behaviors without deliberation. Aquinas attests, "Man does many things without deliberation, which is the case whenever he thinks of nothing, as when someone intent on something else moves his feet or hands or scratches his beard." One could imagine that these "acts of a human" could engender habits within us. Such habits, however, are ordinarily entangled with a significant part of human life—namely, the emotions. We share them with higher animals.

Higher Animals and Purely Emotional Habits

On May 22, 2020, in the midst of the COVID-19 crisis, the Pakistani high court declared that Kaavan would be free. Called "the world's loneliest elephant," pictures of Kaavan in chains had begun to circulate on the internet in 2016. That year, the pop singer Cher began a campaign to free the elephant from its chains and solitude. Well-known as a gay icon and staunch supporter of abortion, Cher sent her personal representative Mark Cowne to the Islamabad zoo to improve Kaavan's living conditions. Four years later, they were victorious. Soon the suffering animal will be relocated to a sanctuary in Cambodia.

On Twitter, Cher exuberantly said, "THIS IS ONE OF THE GREATEST MOMENTS OF MY LIFE. CANT STOP [crying emoji], [smile face with hearts emoji], BEING SICK 2 MY STOMACH. (ATE [cake emoji] in The night & Was SOOO Sick, Still am.Can you O.D. from too much [cake emoji])!? BUT [elephant emoji] KAVAAN IS FREE [prayer hands emoji] [tears emoji] DOWN MY CHEEKS,BUT HES FREE." A fitting tribute to her efforts on behalf of the despondent pachyderm.

As far as I know, there have been no such efforts on behalf of jellyfish, even though they can live up to twenty-five years in captivity. The reason is obvious: elephants are a higher form of animal. In addition to possessing the powers of sensation, perception, and motion, higher animals also possess the mysterious faculty of emotion.

For a few centuries, philosophers thought of animals as meat machines, and psychologists often discounted the interior life and feelings of non-humans. In our time, more and more people recognize with Aquinas that some animals are "higher" than others because they are capable of more perfect functions of memory, estimation, and the affective responses we call emotions. Ethologists have gathered abundant proof that higher animals such as octopi, parrots, and mammals in general display a greater variety of cognitive processes and emotion. Elephants, for instance, manifest panic when they are lost and separated from their herd; they show fear in response to the shape, sound, and smell of lions; their young display playfulness when rolling in the mud; the males, especially those with boosted testosterone, flaunt aggressiveness; and, famously in the case of Kaavan, those who have lost kin or a kin-substitute exhibit sadness. To grasp the existence of animal emotions, however, one can look nearer to home than Mount Kilimanjaro. All a dog owner needs to do is tell Fido that it's time to take a walk, and he'll witness canine emotions at work.

We can describe emotions well enough, but to define them, we must exercise precision. Let us notice, first, that an emotion does not simply happen. We do not feel excited or fearful without cause. Something gives rise to our emotions: one feels excited about a friend's presence, or fearful of a snake. An emotion is "about" something. It is a reaction to some perceived object: an antecedent that triggers it. Felt sensations such as pressure, temperature, brightness, loudness, and physical pleasure or pain often trigger emotions, but sensations are not equivalent to emotions. One might feel mere physical pain from stepping on a tack, or one might feel *pain and anger* from stepping on a child's misplaced LEGO toy. Other times, an emotion can be triggered without immediate sensation. One's *imagination* of a friend's betrayal could conjure up baseless fears; a dog's *estimation* of a postman's threat could elicit anger and barking; a cat's *memory* of tuna in a tin can could prompt desire and meowing. Hence, emotions are not interior perceptions either.

Put succinctly, when an antecedent (A) initiates a higher animal's behavior (B), the animal not only can sense (S) the antecedent and perceive it (P) but also can have an *emotional reaction* to it (E), which could lead to movement (M) and a consequence (C). Here is a simple model of that process:

2. Higher animals

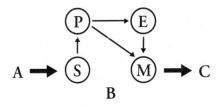

This model shows that higher animals have all the powers of lower animals, with an additional emotional power added to it.

What is an emotion? Here we must distinguish between its material and formal elements, which are like a) the metal of a coin and b) the image stamped onto it.

The material element of emotion comprises the physiological responses an animal has upon estimating an antecedent object's relative benefit or harm. As noted previously, the antecedent could be something presently sensed, or it could exist solely within the imagination or memory. On the neuronal level, a sensation activates particular regions of the brain and, somewhat independently, the autonomic nervous system which helps regulate feelings of calm or alarm. Chemical correlates of emotions have increasingly entered popular discourse, as when one speaks about neurotransmitters such as oxytocin as the "cuddle chemical," or the "dopamine hit" that results from rewarding behaviors, or the endorphins that inundate experienced runners on a long haul. Testosterone is generally linked with masculine aggression, and estrogen with feminine mating strategies. Equally important is how depleted serotonin is related to depression and exploratory behaviors, and cortisol's role in emotions of anxiety and fear. These chemical reactions influence, and are influenced by, changes in the blood, glandular, and gut systems. More visibly, changes occur in skeletal-musculature posture and in the skin, especially in facial expressions. All of these bodily movements and interactions can be more or less coordinated in an emotion. Such integration is possible only because of the formal aspect.

An emotion's formal aspect, put simply, is its basic pattern, quality, and objective meaning. Just as the formal aspect of a coin is the form or shape with which the metal has been stamped, so the formal aspect of an emotion is the patterned physiological movement that arises in response to a perception. Randolph Nesse argues that emotions are differentiated by the way they help a person cope with "related but somewhat different situation[s]." Aquinas more precisely explains that emotions are distinguished by the sorts of objects to which they respond. The term *emotion* comes from the Latin *ex-movere*, literally, "to move away from" something. That *something* is the antecedent object. After sensing an object, an animal performs the cognitive work of estimating an object's benefit or harm. That estimative judgment activates the animal's affective and appetitive power, eliciting an emotion that corresponds to the object-as-cognized.

How many emotions are there? Nesse remarks, "Each emotion has a 'prototype,' that is, characteristics that describe an exemplar at the center of a cloud of somewhat varying responses. These clouds have overlapping blurry boundaries." A Thomist could say that though the objects and situations in the world are unquantifiably diverse, they fall into a small number of formal categories. These correlate to the basic kinds of emotions.

Good is ultimately attractive, and evil is repulsive. The most basic emotion is some sort of love for the good. Every other basic emotion is fundamentally oriented to love as the first movement of the desiring or "seeking" power of an animal (called the "concupiscible appetite" by Aquinas). If a higher animal estimates that the perceived object is beneficial, it typically feels a sort of love for the thing in general, or desire if it is far away, and a sort of joy if it is near. On the other hand, if it perceives the object as harmful, the desiring power has a negative polarity: an animal might feel a sort of dislike for it, or aversion if it is distant, and sadness if it is near.

Secondarily, some basic emotions are more directly activated by the "assertive" power of the animal (called the "irascible appetite" by Aquinas). These emotions urge an animal to assert itself in regard to an object perceived as difficult to obtain or avoid. If the object is good and difficult to obtain, the animal feels hope. When reaching that good seems impossible, the emotion of despair results. If the object appears bad and difficult to avoid, the animal may feel courage if it estimates a win in a fight is possible, or fear if it estimates it will fail, and anger as striving for vindication of threat or harm.

Here is the schema proposed by Aquinas:

	Basic response	Far from agent	Near to agent
Desiring: *simple good*	Love	Desire	Joy
Desiring: *simple evil*	Hate	Aversion	Sadness
Assertive: *difficult good*		*Possible*: Hope	
		Impossible: Despair	
Assertive: *difficult evil*		*Overpowering*: Fear	*Seeking vindication*: Anger
		Overcomable: Confidence	

The upshot is that higher animals exhibit all of these emotions to some degree. Even less intelligent animals such as chickens have rudimentary forms of basic emotions. I saw this for myself when I was in my early teens and visited my grandparents' farm. Once, a chicken died from fright from the mere shadow and smell of a fox. If I stood as still as a whisper inside of a large coop, the chickens showed curiosity and desire, and cautiously hopped forward to give me a peck and see what I tasted like. After the hundreds of chickens were caught, we found a little chick who hid under the sawdust. I named him Ralph. The poor fella acted list-less and floppy—one might have said "sad"—until we were able to introduce him to cheerful puppies who kept him company. Later, Ralph would follow them around, eat their chow, sleep in their kennel, and crow when they would bark. Ralph thought he was a dog. I said chickens aren't too smart.

The higher an animal is, the more perfectly it can be habituated. A good trainer realizes that each animal should be trained within its own limits and individual character-istics. Chickens can be taught to return to a coop at night, to lay eggs in a particular location, and to peck keys on a keyboard. In behaviorist language, to train an animal, you have to train to associate the desired behavior with some reward—for example, pecking keys with a bit of grain.

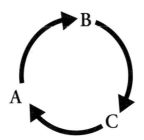

- *Antecedent*: light on piano key
- *Behavior*: chicken pecks the key
- *Consequent*: reward of grain

A Thomistic perspective would point out that this sort of habituation is effective because it shapes the chicken's estimative power to judge that the desired behavior—peck-ing keys—is good for it in that moment. Habituation and learning are closely intertwined, even if the learning does not entail insight or understanding of what is happening. A chicken does not know it is plinking out the tune of "The Star-Spangled Banner"; it is probably not patriotic. But it does perceive that grain is worth eating, and it estimates it can receive grain by pecking at keys in a certain order.

Because emotions are *reactions* to situations, an animal cannot entirely control its emotions. Aquinas states that emotions "have their own proper movements" and practically "have a will of their own," because they are guided by the partly-voluntary habits of instinct and estimative judgment. Nevertheless, the emotions of animals can be habituated to some degree. Suppose a dog regularly barks at a visitor out of anger and fear. To teach a dog not to bark, an owner might associate the barking with a punishment such as closing the dog in a room—thereby habituating the dog to estimate that barking is somehow to be avoided. Or the owner might calm his dog with reassuring words and give the dog a treat when it ceases barking—thereby habituating the dog to estimate that being friendly toward the visitor is rewarding.

Techniques of animal training have huge implications for our emotional habits. Before we address that issue, however, we must consider habits of the intellect and will.

The Human Animal and Intellectual-Volitional Habits

Nature literature is fraught with anthropomorphism, whereby animal lovers attribute human emotions and thoughts to other animals. It's not unusual for an experienced zoologist to put words into the maws of familiar creatures. Here's a typical example: a large bull elephant approaches a female elephant, and a writer describes the scene: "They rumble and briefly wrap trunks. . . . Then he pauses, just standing there with an almost exaggerated nonchalance, his gigantic trunk draped over a massive tusk. 'It's to show females, "I'm not so scary; look how relaxed and casual I am." We actually call it "being casual,"' Vicki [the ethologist] tells me."

Vicki might be correctly interpreting the elephant's behavior, but it does not follow that the animals use words to understand and describe its own behavior, or that they have some sort of rationality. Animal lovers might mean well, but it is rather silly to say "animals are people too." Animals never say that. They can't say that. It's exactly backwards. Humans are animals too: *rational* animals. As Aquinas states, animals and humans do not differ in animality but rather in the rational principle that we have over and above animality. We share some traits and powers in common with beasts, but not rationality.

You may have noticed that I have avoided saying that animals think or judge. My choice of language was intentional: those words are too vague to sort out whether human intelligence is categorically different from that of apes, elephants, octopi, and dolphins. Animals act non-rationally. They must, for they cannot reason, have insight, or think abstractly. Aquinas explains the difference between beast-knowledge and human-knowledge by positing that the terms *intellect* and *intelligence* come from the Latin *intus legere*, meaning, "to read within." Sensory knowledge is concerned with exterior qualities (whether present, imagined, or remembered), whereas intelligent understanding penetrates into the very essence of a thing. British analytic philosopher P. M. S. Hacker explains that the power of reason includes the *ability to apprehend reasons*, such as reasons for things being "thus and so," reasons for ends (and hence for wanting something), reasons for one's feelings and emotions, and reasons for action and omission. Animal behavior may be purposeful, but their behavior and communicative sounds—even complex elephant grunts or dolphin chatter—do not demonstrate they apprehend reasons *for* anything. Hacker wisely observes, "Non-language-using animals . . . can have purposes. But animals cannot reason their way to the adoption of a purpose; they cannot weigh the reasons for and against what they do or what they aim at, or give reasons justifying or explaining their behavior to themselves or others."

It follows that "animals cannot deliberate, ruminate or reflect, let alone draw inferences, derive conclusions or deduce consequences—only recognize, associate, learn and anticipate."

In contrast, humans can apprehend reasons such as those listed above, and we can debate the rightness of those reasons. Our concepts transcend particular and perceptible objects. In addition to be able to imagine or remember lilies and cougars, we can conceive of imperceptible objects such as mathematical theorems and quarks; we can philosophize about very abstract ideas such as truth and aesthetics; we can posit the existence of entirely spiritual things, such as angels and God. With our intellects, we can know the essences of things, affirm or deny the truth of a proposition, deliberately focus on an abstract idea, and understand and explain the natures of things.

Integrated with the intellect, the will is the other faculty of our spiritual soul. In addition to the natural appetite or desire that lower animals have, and in addition to the sensory desires of the emotions, there is the will. Aquinas calls it the "rational appetite." By the will, we can move ourselves to pursue the good, or to avoid and flee evil, as we understand it. Knowledge and understanding grasped by the intellect informs the will. Directed by the mind, the will then wishes, intends, chooses, and if the good is achieved, enjoys it. Just as one of the chief tasks of the intellect is to ask "Why?" about something, and to grasp the end for-the-sake-of-which one should act, so one of the chief tasks of the will is to *intend* the end, especially the ultimate end, which one grasps as good for oneself.

There is a certain freedom of action in the will because one can will or not-will when one so chooses. Furthermore, the intellect's power enables us to step back from sensations and images and consider them rationally. Our minds, rightly used, free us from the tyranny of instincts, emotions, and guesstimates. Unlike chimps and their zoo pals, we can choose to follow the urges of our sub-rational powers—or choose to walk a path less travelled. Here is how the intellect and will relate to the lower powers:

In this case, the intellect (I) receives information from the perception (P) and has a potential back-and-forth influence with the will (V), which can command the perceptions as well as motor powers (M). There is an arrow proceeding from the intellect and entering it because the intellect can think about itself and all its content. Similarly, the arrow proceeding from the will back to itself indicates that the will can move itself and choose to approve or disapprove of its previous choices. This allows for true self-reflexivity.

3. Humans

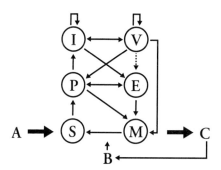

The intellect and will make humans different from the rest of the animals, and this makes a huge difference to our habituation. Hacker notes, "A being that can act for reasons is *responsible* for its actions. To be responsible . . . for one's actions is to be answerable for what one does. And that is precisely what non-language-using animals are not. For only if one *can* answer can one be answerable."

Because we are rational animals, we are born into responsibility as a natural inheritance. Nemesius, a fourth-century bishop, put it this way: unlike the behavior of beasts, a human act that is performed with anger or desire, or any other emotion, remains intentional, since if the action is right, a person wants praise, but if wrong, he is blamed. This is because a human act originates primarily from within the agent, and "it was in their power not to be easily trapped by their emotions: such things are corrected by habit." St.

Thomas goes a step further and argues that human habits not only are helpful for avoiding extreme emotionalism but also are *necessary* for our full perfection.

A habit is a quality that shapes a particular power. When a habit is in accord with that power and the object that affects it, the habit is good and perfective. The highest human habits are those which exist in that which makes us most human—that is, in the intellect and will. Now, the object of the intellect is truth. When the intellect regularly grasps its proper object—truth—it becomes habituated to beholding the truth. The mind becomes stamped by the truth, much like the metal of a coin is stamped with the head of a sovereign. This quality of being formed by the truth is good for the intellect. When the intellect has this quality, it is all the stronger for it: a truth-shaped mind can more easily sift through rumor, reject falsehood, discover reality, and so on. Accordingly, the habit of grasping the truth quickly, easily, skillfully, and joyfully *is* the perfection of the intellect. Seen from the other end of things, when the intellect is properly habituated, it grasps the truth so quickly, easily, etc. that knowledge, insight, understanding, and the rest seem natural to it. The contrary also holds. Falsehood and fantasy weaken the mind, preparing it to wander, darkened, lost in a maze of misshapen mirrors. Gazing into the black hole of unreality destabilizes the intellect and deprives it of the light of truth. Like the men turned to stone by looking at Medusa, the mind that habitually fixes itself on lies becomes hardened to the splendor of reality.

A similar dynamic exists with the will. Its proper object is the authentic good. When the will continually chooses what is truly good, it becomes stronger, more energetic, more stable, more excellent in its choices and loves. Likewise, when the will rejects what is evil and shuns the corruption of immorality, it comes to love and appreciate the good even more—much as a gardener who chases off fruit-eating birds can make his cherry tree flourish more abundantly. On the other hand, fake goods disguised as real goods are to the will as drugs are to the body: at first, they might bring pleasure, but in the long run, they destroy the power from within, fostering addiction, weakness, pettiness, and, eventually, hatred of what is truly beneficial. Again, when a person's desires are not in accord with what is truly good, this perversion of the rational appetite destroys the harmonious balance of a man's interior life, similar to how cancer destroys the body from the inside out.

Our habits take us either downward or upward. When a person's intellect is habituated to what is false, and his will to what is evil, his soul is corrupted, and he lives with the inclinations of a brutish animal like a pig. It is like one of those movies where two people switch bodies, but in this case, the human soul is switched with that of a pig. On the other hand, when a person develops good habits to an extraordinary degree, the soul is perfected. To anticipate future chapters, if by grace one's habits exceed the usual human mode, the soul becomes heroic or even divine by participation in God's own perfection. But how does such habit formation relate to the emotions? Can we habituate the emotions themselves?

Emotional Habits for Humans

To understand emotional habits for humans, we can turn to Plato. He was the first Western thinker to discuss the soul (*psuché*) in terms of its rational foundation (*logos*). In other words, he initiated the study of psychology. Plato offers a number of helpful images of the soul; here, I focus on one in his great dialogue, the *Republic*.

Imagine one of those grotesque creatures that legends tell us used to exist in ancient times, Plato suggests. Visualize the monsters in which many different kinds of things grow naturally into one, such as a griffin (an eagle and lion) or Pegasus (a horse with wings). Now, envisage three creatures. The first and biggest is a hydra with many heads—some gentle, some savage beasts. The second and next in size is a lion. The third is a human. Somehow fuse these three into one creature. Finally, cover them all with the skin of a human being so that anyone who looks at the thing sees only the outer covering and thinks that it is a single creature, a human. That is an image of the soul. We can interpret this three-fold image of the soul in light of Aquinas's division of appetites.

The multi-headed hydra corresponds to the desiring (concupiscible) appetite: the many heads, and their many mouths, symbolize the many different desires we possess. Some desires are gentle like the cow, such as the desire for melodious sounds or delicious smells. Other desires are fierce, such as the desires for reproduction and honor.

The lion corresponds to the assertive (irascible) appetite. For the ancients, lions typified whatever was strong, courageous, and noble. The assertive appetite has similar qualities.

It is strong because it seeks to achieve difficult goods and to overcome difficult evils; it possesses the natural emotions of hope and confidence, which aid courage; and by seeking a rectification of evil through vindication, it displays a sort of nobility.

Then there is the human. The interior aspect of the human represents the rational appetite, the will. Although the will exists somehow alongside the desiring and assertive appetites, it is the only one that looks human. This represents how the rational power—both intellect and will—is most proper to a human, that which distinguishes Adam from the beasts. Through the deliberate action of the will, the person is able to rationally choose the good and the beautiful.

Plato's image magnificently illustrates how the different aspects of the soul can be either in conflict or in harmony with each other. By depicting the various sources of desire as separate animals, Plato shows how these desires have a sort of independence from each other. Furthermore, he shows why our interior war is unequal, and why our better reason is often the loser: the desiring appetite is larger and has powers of self-generation and shapeshifting. Just when you cut off one head of non-rational desire, another springs up in its place. Just when you think you have tamed a desire, it grows fangs and spits poison. The assertive part, symbolized by the lion, is between the hydra and the man: sometimes we can feel angry at our lower desires, or angry at oneself for being enslaved by them. Sometimes the assertive appetite urges us to take vengeance against our desires through penance or even self-harm. Finally, there is the human part, naturally superior, more intelligent than the other creatures, but somehow weaker. As more reasonable, it possesses the natural right and duty to rule the other parts of the soul. When it succeeds in its task, there is harmony. When it fails, emotion and disordered desire chaotically fight for precedence.

Aquinas offers two basic reasons why our various appetites are often at odds with one another. First, the vast difference between matter and spirit entails that they can operate somewhat independently within a single person. Clearly, the "vegetative" powers work on their own, for the autonomic nervous system naturally regulates functions such as blood circulation, breathing, digestion, and so on. These cannot be directly commanded by reason. The lower powers of animals can operate without reason as well. Eyes receive light, ears receive sound, skin receives sensations of pressure and temperature, and so on, naturally. Sense impressions in turn activate the proper movements of animal higher powers— that is, the interior sensory powers of imagination, memory, and estimation. The sight of a looming pine tree, for instance, could activate a recollection of trees near your parent's house in childhood. A creaking sound could initiate an imaginative fear of ghosts creeping down the hall. The features of a speaker's face could induce an estimation that the person is dangerous and untrustworthy. These are natural, organic processes that do not require the will's intervention. Consequently, the movements of the sensory powers can elicit the desiring or assertive appetites. Aquinas states, "The sensitive appetite is naturally moved not only . . . in man by the cogitative [estimative] power which the universal reason guides, but also by the imagination and sense." That is why we sometimes feel love without meaning to, or anger despite ourselves. Aquinas notes that we experience how these emotional movements fight against reason "to the extent that we sense or imagine something pleasurable that reason forbids, or something unpleasant that reason commands." The multi-headed hydra can lick its chops before the lion becomes indignant and reason intervenes.

Second, one's reason lacks consistent harmony with one's imagination, memory, estimation, and emotions because of sin. In a later chapter, I will do a deep dive into how sin affects habituation. Here, we may note that before Adam and Eve ripped apart the chain of command by their fault, our lower powers had been as well-behaved as the animals were in Eden. When the world was created, all was in order through the grace of original justice. This grace was a supernatural habit infused into their souls, one which ordered the body to the soul, and the soul to God. If any movement of the body arose independently of deliberate choice, that movement was nevertheless good, for it was guided by the grace that always ordered the entire person to the ultimate good. When Adam and Eve sinned, however, they lost this grace for themselves and for the rest of us. The first sour note in harmonious nature was sounded by original sin. The body was no longer ordered to the rational good but to the sensory good; it was no longer directed to heaven but to earth. Additionally, original and personal sin harm one's virtuous inclinations: wickedness makes our good desires stumble, or knocks them down altogether.

Gregory the Great argues that "the movements of the flesh" are like beasts, for, "while they gall the mind by prompting conduct contrary to reason, [they] rise up against us like beasts. But when the heart is bowed down under the Divine Law, even the incitements of the flesh are reduced, so that, though in tempting us they give a low growl, yet they never mount so high as to the execution of the deeds, as to the madness of open biting." He then points to the great apostle to show how everyone is beset by these beasts in some way. St. Paul admitted that he suffered from an inner tension as part of himself warred with another part. He said, "I do not do the good I want, but the evil I do not want is what I do. . . . For I delight in the law of God, in my inmost self, but I see in my members another law at war with the law of my mind and making me captive to the law of sin which dwells in my members" (Rom 7:19, 22–23). Interpretations of these famed phrases vary; here, I follow Aquinas.

According to Aquinas, St. Paul lamented that his will delighted in God through charity, as his mind was ruled by faith, whereas his animal appetites, which dwelt in his body, were still moved by the law of sin. St. Thomas explains, "The inclination to sin is a punishment for the fault of sins . . . [for] sin, which has taken mastery over the sinner and imposed its law on him, namely, the inclination to sin, just as a master imposes his law on a vanquished slave." He also notes that just as "fierceness" can be considered a sort of law for dogs and "meekness" a sort of law for sheep as expressions of their natural inclinations, so a person who turns his back on God falls under the influence of his sensual impulses similar to those of animals. In sub-human animals, that inclination-law is in accord with their nature, and good. But in humans, that inclination-law is often a deviation and insubordination to the law of reason, and thus fights against his nature, strips him of his proper dignity, and makes him a slave of his lower cravings. Adam and Eve gave us the habitual inclination toward selfishness and away from God, which we call original sin. Our personal sins add further bad habits that turn us in on self and away from the highest good. No wonder that we all feel as if we are at war with ourselves.

Taming Your Habits

Inside you is a hydra, a lion, and a human. They battle for preeminence, struggling to win control of the outer man. How do you address this situation?

The multi-headed monster is biggest, and often the strongest. The desire for good is the foundation of all our emotions and actions. When we are united with a desired good and feel pleasure, we will be more inclined to perform corresponding acts in the future; we will also be more attached to that good. Studies suggest that "the mammal brain scans constantly for potential rewards, and dopamine is the signal that it has found some." More precisely, when a person is habituated to delighting in a particular person, object, or action, the neurotransmitter chemicals dopamine and oxytocin further engrain the positive experience into our brains. In other words, there is a strong pleasure-habit connection. This natural process is meant to unite us to the good.

But when this process is directed to things that are better suited for beasts, it can make our life descend into chaos. The interior hydra works to gain dominance within you by gobbling up more and more objects: each time you indulge your desires thoughtlessly, especially for pleasure and self-satisfaction, you feed the hydra within. Then the habits of the desiring appetite, without the direction of reason, gain greater power. Analyzed through the habit loop, we see the following:

- *Antecedent*: a good perceived as desirable
- *Behavior*: indulging the desire without intervention of reason
- *Consequent*: strengthened appetite of desire

Eventually, your desires can become so strong that they overcome your self-critical side and pull your reason along wide paths down to darkness and destruction. In time, reason, captured by the hydra and tormented by the lion, undergoes Stockholm syndrome and rationalizes that the hydra was right the whole time. This is why addicts of various sorts often find it difficult to see anything wrong with their behavior and have little desire to change their habits until they fall into the holes they have dug for themselves.

The lion is smaller than the hydra but nobler and therefore more persuasive because it natively combats evil wherever it might be found. After perceiving insult or injury, threatened or actual, your interior lion responds by restoring order, thereby preserving yourself and the goods you care for. This sort of behavior could be appealing because such victories seemingly preserve your well-being and everything connected to it:

- *Antecedent*: approaching harm
- *Behavior*: restoration of order through self-assertion
- *Consequent*: intensified assertive, irascible appetite

When the habit of the assertive appetite is intensified and strengthened without reason, the result is an upward spiral of power for the interior lion. If the lion becomes king of the soul's jungle, mastering the hydra and the human, it will prowl about the world looking for evil to devour. Everything starts to look like prey. Not only will the lion growl at the annoyances and wickedness of others; it will also turn on the self, attempting to bite the heads off of the hydra and the human. Such wild lions can be let loose in individuals and in crowds. Wordsworth lamented the masses who were manipulated into becoming furious mobs:

> Lost people, trained to theoretic feud! . . .
> Lost above all, ye labouring multitude!
> In burst of outrage spread your judgements wide,
> And to your wrath cry out, "Be thou our guide."

Unchecked anger strives to destroy whatever is in its path: your neighbors, your desires, your rationality, even the whole world if power were afforded to it. When it gains supreme mastery within, your assertiveness transforms into aggression, aggression becomes violence, violence leads to hate, and hate breeds death. Perhaps this is why it has been said that we should distrust all in whom the impulse to punish is powerful. Reason at the service of the irascible appetites depicts oneself as a righteous crusader for justice when, in actuality, one becomes a knight in Satan's service.

Smaller than the hydra, with less prowess than the lion, the human nevertheless is wiser. The human lifts up his head. How should he address the monster and the beast within?

This chapter began with a story of a dog nipping at my heels while I was on a run. The story speaks to animal emotions and human reason. It illustrates not only human-beast relations in the lawn of life but also our inner workings, and it suggests how to harness our appetites and habits. How you react to a snarling pup helps you see how to respond to your lower powers. Here are the options.

1. *Ignore them.* When faced with a mean dog, many people are tempted to run away. Similarly, when encountering an emotional difficulty, a common response is to avoid whatever triggered it—and even to turn away from the emotion itself. People who feel overwhelmed by their fear, anger, attraction, etc. may want to deny the emotion itself, judging it as harmful and therefore as something to be shunned. They hope that neglect will make it go away: don't water a passion with attention, and maybe it will wilt. This sort of reaction might be effective for small, temporary, and fairly meaningless feelings, but it is not a lifetime solution. Some emotions, like some animals, will run and catch up with you unless you deal with it directly. Furthermore, because emotions are part of our very selves, if we run away from them, we will never achieve personal integration. Aquinas insists that human perfection means the perfection of our whole person: not just our minds and wills but also our passions. If we distance ourselves from our lower powers, our monstrous and bestial aspects will fight for dominance on a typically subconscious level. And they will often win.

2. *Cage them.* If you can't ignore a dangerous animal, you could try to lock it up. This option is gaining more popularity as irrationality and emotionality increasingly dominate life. Fearful and assertive people often agree on this: they are attracted to the idea of controlling wily emotions by putting them into a box. If you feel tirelessly chased by your passion, they might say, lock it up until it starves to death. Such was the view of the quintessential Stoics, who offered many reasons for caging the emotions: tranquility from no longer fighting with oneself, greater dignity through self-control, and the circumvention of dangers from feelings running wild. The chief problem with this so-called solution is that emotions are part of ourselves: similar to the avoidance technique, the cage technique could easily lead to a psychologically split self, or what some call suppression. Furthermore, because emotion is natural, when a person tries to cage the hydra and lion, the result becomes like an underfed, neglected zoo animal that will not die: the poor thing gets weaker, and perhaps more unruly, but it endures. The result is apathy, the dissipation of all motivation, and, worse, athymia—a flat, grey world devoid of emotional flavor and color. It is little surprise that after a person feels her imagination, hope, love, confidence, and anger has been caged, she desires to set them all free.

3. *Uncage them.* Romantic poetry, literature, and thought luxuriates in passions unfettered from

reason and polite society, portraying sympathetic
scenes in which reason needs to let them loose
to whirl about in nature. Dystopian novels also
often include forebodings of a future in which
authoritarian governments stifle the sharp flavor of
true passion and replace it with chemical substitutes.
"Stability," insists the Controller in Huxley's *Brave
New World*. "No civilization without social stability.
No social stability without individual stability. . . .
The primal and ultimate need." As a result, the
totalitarian government scientists work to "preserve"
all people from having any significant emotions.
Throwing off these repressive structures, romantics
of one sort or another strive to let feelings fly. A
tragic-heroic character in *Brave New World* says to
the Controller, "I don't want comfort. I want God,
I want poetry, I want real danger, I want freedom, I
want goodness. I want sin." Other main characters
are portrayed as finding their humanity through
sexual intercourse outside of government control.
A similar narrative unfolds in Orwell's *Nineteen
Eighty-Four*. While rightly holding that emotion is
a part of human nature, and that healthy emotions
ought to be expressed, the narratives fail by placing
passion above reason, by suggesting that all emotion
is good emotion, and by loosing the person from all
moral structure, resulting in moral emptiness.

4. *Hurt them.* When uncaged emotions bite, the
reaction of some is to give them a whack. Sometimes
this is because people do not want, nor do they like,

the independence of emotions: they expect emotions to act with the crystalline clarity of pure logic. They want their feelings to be their docile slaves; they want the power to elicit or suppress anger, fear, and love the way they can move an arm or leg. It is reasonable, of course, to wish that emotions were in accordance with reason. But it is an error to treat emotions as if they had no independence or life of their own. Temple Grandin, an autistic expert in animal behavior and emotions, illustrates the issue vividly. She recounts how a person who had a pet lion shipped it on an airplane: "Someone thought the lion might like to have a pillow for the trip, the way people do, so they gave him one, and the lion ate it and died. The point [is]: don't be anthropomorphic. It's dangerous to the animal." We should not attribute our thoughts to our emotions, and we should not expect emotions to be in accord with our reasoning until we have used our minds to act reasonably. Undoubtedly, there may be occasions to indulge an emotion, just as you might need to help a lion sleep, and there are other occasions for fighting an emotion when it threatens your overall well-being, similar to giving a dog shock-therapy to stop its attack. These are at best short-term solutions to an immediate problem. You will no more have healthy emotions by merely whipping them than you will get good behavior from a dog solely by spanking it. Furthermore, it's not very effective. Beating a beast or using some other severe punishment does not change its nature.

It is thoughtless folly to allow one's emotions to run rampant through the field of life, but to torture oneself over one's previous passions, to be overly cast down by the weight of sadness, to be depressed by the sting of one's former blind emotions—and then to whip oneself and others in a fit of anger—is also folly. Even Nietzsche could see this when he warned, "Whoever fights monsters should see to it that in the process he does not become a monster."

5. *Tame them.* The last, and best, option for dealing with the emotions, as with dangerous animals, is to tame them. What does it mean to tame the emotions? In a phrase, it means to habituate them to right reason's good influence.

Reason relates to the emotions as a ruler relates to citizens within a city. This idea was articulated by Plato in his *Republic*, adopted by Aristotle in his *Politics*, and developed by Aquinas. The medieval friar summarizes: "The Philosopher says (*Politics* I, c. 2) that the reason governs the irascible and concupiscible not by a 'despotic rule,' which is that of a master over his slave; but by a 'politic and royal rule,' whereby the free are governed, who are not wholly subject to command."

Royal rule is that of a king who cares for his citizens and acts for their good. Rather than seeking only his own good, as does a despot, a good monarch considers the common good that is shared by all the citizens and himself. He does this through "political rule," which exercises power not in an unlimited way but as restricted by the laws of the particular city. In classic Venice, the doge governed the water-bound republic only in conjunction with the families who belonged to the "Great Council." In England, restrictions were placed upon the king by the nobles who induced him to sign the *Magna Carta* in 1215.

Applying this political lesson to habituation, we see that reason governs the interior senses and emotions according to their own "proper laws"—that is, according to their nature in general as bodily powers that respond to environmental stimuli and according to how they exist within the particular person. The more a person works against his lower nature, the more the habits will be disordered. But the more reason guides and shapes the lower powers in accord with their natures, the more easily they can become habituated to the end which reason sets before them.

Such is the basis of much animal training. A German shepherd can be trained in a K-9 unit to be very docile and friendly toward its master but aggressive in response to a spoken cue. When *habituation as training* underlies an animal's behavior, the reason behind the action comes from the trainer. The animal's estimation, emotions, and behavior participate in the rational agency of the trainer. When a human becomes habituated to a right behavior, and to a reasonable emotional response, his lower powers participate in his intellect and will in a greater way than can sub-human animals. Whereas an animal may share in the goals and understanding of the trainer, it nevertheless acts *non-rationally* since it acts from habituated instinct without understanding the essence or the final goal of what it is doing. In contrast, when we set our intention on the right end, our lower powers come to possess the same end and become "rationalized." This is where Plato's image of a three-fold creature—hydra, lion, and man—breaks down, for those are only metaphors for aspects of ourselves that are naturally and organically united.

When we habituate our emotions rightly, we develop those virtues that are nothing other than perfections of emotional faculties. The virtue of temperance perfects our desiring appetite, and the virtue of fortitude perfects our assertive appetite. These virtues are the habits that have shaped our appetites in such a way that we respond emotionally to situations, but with emotion that is informed and guided by reason perfected through the virtue of prudence and chosen rightly by the will perfected through the virtue of justice.

Techniques for training animals can help us when they are adapted to the needs of our nature as *rational* animals. Many of these techniques are related to the simple habit loop discussed previously. To ensure that our habits shape not only our behavior but our soul, we should also have recourse to Aquinas's insights about the object and end of a human act. In other words, to tame our passions and develop virtue within ourselves, we must appeal to our higher nature by considering motives of the best sort.

The saints illustrate how good habits strengthen both the particular faculty in which the habit resides and the person as a whole. Consider the case of St. Thomas More. Often he is praised, even by non-Catholics, for his fidelity to conscience despite great pressure. Implicitly recognized is that More's adherence to his convictions was not mere stubbornness. Obstinate willfulness was not why he rejected the validity of Henry VIII's adulterous marriage and the oath which proclaimed Henry's supremacy over the Church. Rather, More held to his judgment because he was convinced that Henry's claims were false. He could remain steadfast because he had habituated himself—with the help of grace—to loving and seeking the truth, and to holding it fast whenever it came within his grasp. Throughout his life, he had been assiduous in prayer and in studying the Catholic faith. Whether pouring over works of Augustine, contemplating Sacred Scripture, or composing defenses of Catholic doctrines against Lutheranism, he was like the prophet who ate the book and found it as sweet as honey. By the time the question of Henry's claims arose, More's intellect was so habitually fixed on the truth that he was receptive to God's kindly light even in the damp, dark cell that overlooked the place of execution. A deep, ongoing encounter with reality so strengthened More's mind and will that he preferred to lose his head rather than lose the truth.

More's example, and that of all the saints in their heroic virtue, illustrates another quality of good habits of the intellect and will: they bring order and even peace to the emotions. While awaiting execution in 1535, More penned a long work entitled *A Dialogue of Comfort against Tribulation*, therein discussing among other things how the right habitual frame of mind and will can pacify the emotions. He wrote: "Even the fear of a very shameful and painful death allows for an increase or diminishment of dread, depending on the different affections that are previously fixed and rooted in the mind. This is true to an amazing extent. . . . And I don't doubt but that you have heard many well-authenticated stories of people who for one cause or another have not hesitated to suffer death quite willingly—different ones in different ways, but some in both physical torment and humiliating disgrace."

Thomas More explained that "affections become imprinted in people's minds," sometimes by bodily sensations, when they are offered something pleasant or unpleasant. At other times, a person develops affections through reason: "in an orderly way, reason tempers those affections which are imprinted by the five bodily senses. Often it disposes a person toward some spiritual virtues that run very contrary to those fleshly, sensual affections. These reason-based dispositions, or spiritual affections," or *good habits of the soul*, "are proper to human nature; they are above the nature of animals." More went on to say that the devil and the Holy Spirit compete to plant the different affections within us, and depending on who we cooperate with, one or the other type will be watered and take root, eventually bearing fruit in time of trial. If sensory habits dominate our soul, then we shall be weaker against the terror of death. If an intense love of Christ fills our heart, we shall be stronger against fear.

Utilizing the Thomistic habit loop that we saw in chapter 1, More's example and teaching would look like this:

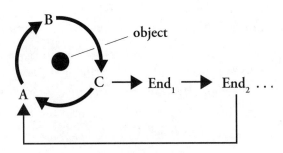

- *Antecedent*: habituated love of God; habituated faith in Catholic teachings
- *Behavior*: refusing to take the Oath of Supremacy
- *Object of the act*: steadfastness in the Catholic faith
- *Consequents*: calmer emotions and greater union with God
- *End₁*: To avoid lying; to be faithful to the truth grasped by conscience
- *End₂*: To see the face of God in heaven
- *Circumstances*: emotions about imprisonment, potential execution, etc.

This model illustrates the same basic dynamic of habituation that we have seen at work elsewhere.

Undoubtedly, More's insight regarding the benefits of good habits was grounded in his own experience. When his daughter, his beloved daughter, the apple of his eye, Margaret, visited him in the Tower of London, she came with a purpose. *Take the oath*, she urged; *save yourself, and come back home to us.* More replied that he must refuse, though doing so cut him deeply. Before making his decision, he said, he pondered many a restless night the peril that could befall him. It was with a "full heavy heart" and imagination running with fear that he determined he must refuse the oath. Margaret did not understand. She could hardly accept it. Thomas More insisted that he *felt* the situation deeply: "Surely Meg, a fainter heart than your frail father has, you cannot have." Nevertheless, he also insisted, "The clearness of my conscience hath made mine heart hop for joy."

More was no übermensch who disdained tears. Nor was he a snowflake who had an emotional meltdown when faced with difficulty. The saint had a profound range of emotions guided by his deep thought, his unshakeable will, and his profound love. Need I point out that this is of an entirely higher order than the calm a bull elephant displays before a potential female conquest?

CHAPTER 4

MINDFUL HABITS

A serpent wrapped itself seven times around the body of Siddhārtha Gautama, called the Buddha. The purpose was not to kill the young man who, according to the ancient manuscripts, had recently received enlightenment underneath a tree. Rather, the serpent, the king of the Nagas, half-human, half-cobra semidivine beings, meant to spread its hood over the Buddha to protect him from the elements of nature. It thought, "Let the 'Blessed One' feel no cold or heat or touch of gadflies, gnats, wind, sun, and creeping things." Freedom from nature enabled the Buddha to declare:

> Disinterest in the world is happiness
> For him that has surmounted these desires.
> But to be rid of the conceit "I am"—
> That is the greatest happiness of all.

To spread this message, the Indian sage taught the way of mindfulness to monks who surrounded him.

Scores of researchers around the world, especially psychologists, have tested the effects of mindfulness. It is not uncommon to read in newspapers or magazines that the practice of mindfulness, and related practices of meditation, can help calm emotion, increase attention, and promote acceptance of

life's sufferings. Such practices often incorporate the fundamental practice of mindfulness, as explained by the Buddha:
non-judgmental awareness of one's body, feelings, mental
activities, and mental objects. The ultimate goal of mindfulness, according to him, is to realize that it is equally true (and
false) to say "I have a Self" and "I have no Self." Perhaps this
is why studies show that, in addition to positive outcomes of
mindfulness, 82 percent of regular practitioners report fear,
anxiety, or paranoia, and a significant portion report a loss of
the sense of one's basic self and a loss of agency.

Mindfulness as understood within its Buddhist context, therefore, is not a "fullness" but an "emptiness." But
mind-emptiness no more perfects the mind than relaxation
strengthens muscles. What is needed is mind*fulness* in the
truer sense of the term: a mind *full* of what perfects it, and
the fullness of the mind at work. Only then will our very
lives be full, complete, and fulfilling. As Aquinas noted,
"Every living thing gives proof of its life by that operation
which is most proper to it and to which it is most inclined.
Thus, the life of plants is said to consist in nourishment
and generation; the life of animals in sensation and movement; and the life of men in their understanding and acting
according to reason."

Jesus Christ is the way to true mindfulness: he offers to
fill the mind with the truth, and he calls his followers to use
their minds fully to reach full perfection. That fullness is
a share in his own divinity. The good Pharisee Nicodemus
said to Jesus, "Rabbi, we know that you are a teacher come
from God" (Jn 3:2). True enough. Christ accepted this title:
"You call me Teacher and Lord; and you are right, for so I

am" (Jn 13:13). But Christ is not merely *from* God; he *is* God. He did not merely teach in words and example, as other men do. Aquinas notes, "Christ also instructs within, because 'He was the true light, which enlightens every man' (Jn 1:9); thus he alone gives wisdom: 'I will give you an eloquence and a wisdom' (Lk 21:15), and this is something that no mere man can say."

As St. Bonaventure beautifully observed, there are three modes of knowing, and Christ is the teacher of each: he is the master of faith, reason, and contemplation, insofar as Christ himself attests, "I am the way, and the truth, and the life" (Jn 14:6). Jesus has a self: he is the author and the teacher, the director and the helper of our intelligence and understanding, for he is the uncreated wisdom of God made visible, the Word of the Father made flesh. God wants us to *believe*, to *know*, and to *contemplate* the truth through Christ, with Christ, and in Christ—and He wants our minds to bear fruit in love for Christ and action performed for Christ. To develop divinely heroic habits, therefore, we must grasp what the mind is, what the mind does, how it goes right, and how it goes wrong.

Distinctions and the Act of Judgment

The Stoics taught their students to calm feelings and improve behavior by reevaluating situations in the light of right reason. Cognitive therapy is similar. It holds that a) thoughts are the primary cause of emotion and behavior; b) thoughts can be known and changed; c) by altering thoughts, one can achieve desired emotional and behavioral change. In sum, change the thoughts, change the man.

These claims are golden apples of wisdom served on a silver platter of simplicity, considering that the mind is the primary source of human uniqueness. When the mind works, it has a top-down effect on everything else we experience, choose, love, and feel. Accordingly, we can learn to manage our emotions better when we are able to *distinguish* among different realities, as well as improve our *reasoning*, so as to achieve better *understanding* about ourselves and the world. Let's consider these acts in turn.

When it comes to forming habits, one of the first activities a person should perform is to distinguish among different kinds of behaviors within himself. In the last chapter, I showed that there are crucial differences among sensations, memories, estimations, emotions, and rational deliberation, as well as their complex interactions. Reason's work of distinguishing between one thing and another, or in determining that two things that seem different are really the same, is called *judgment*. A judgment weighs a proposition, a claim about the state of things, which takes simple forms: "*this* is this, but that is *that*" or "*this* is different than *that*" or "*this* is the same as *that*." Such work is possible when we define our terms well. We can say "I was *sad* but not *depressed*" only if we know what *sad* and *depressed* mean. When feelings are hot and much is at stake, however, proper distinctions and definitions do not always come to mind.

Sometimes people confuse a description with a feeling: "I was so sad because I have been experiencing depression, and I can't feel happy about anything. I cry a lot, and then sit around staring at the ceiling all day." These describe *the same emotion* and related behaviors.

Sometimes people confuse a thought with a feeling: "I was really angry this week because I thought my boss was going to insult me again." At root, this is a *prediction* and an accompanying emotional reaction. The trigger of the emotion was a thought: speculation about the future.

Sometimes people confuse a feeling with two or more thoughts: "I feel like this is the best person to marry and that she will make me happy." The first thought here is a judgment that someone is an optimal marriage choice, and the other is a reason for why the result of the union could be a positive emotion.

More problematic than mere confusion of categories, many believe that some external trigger is sufficient to explain their feelings, thoughts, or behavior. A typical result is blame-shifting. "Of course I was enraged," a rioter might say. "Anyone would be if they were *truly* anti-racist." We commonly make similar assumptions about the emotions of others: "No wonder she felt listless and distressed. She was in lockdown for months." These judgments overlook the fact that people could respond differently to such situations. An anti-racist person could feel an anguished despair instead of anger; a motivated person might enjoy the opportunity afforded by lockdown to pray in silence.

Different reactions are possible because there is a distinction between what Aquinas calls "extrinsic" versus "intrinsic" principles of human action. Both events and bodily reactions to them, such as the first movements of emotions, are "extrinsic" principles of action: they are triggers (or antecedents) that *incline* a person to act. It is important to note that no trigger *causes* or forces us to think about it one way or another. Anyone can experience this for himself, Aquinas argues, for by our thought, we can moderate or even instigate our anger, fear, sadness, and other emotions. Here, the A-B-C pattern of the habit loop may prove useful. It illustrates how events, emotions, thoughts, and acts interact.

Antecedent: event	Belief	Consequence: feeling	Consequence: exterior act
Frank sees food.	He thinks it is good to eat.	Desire	He eats the food.
Frank sees food.	He realizes it is bad for health.	Muted desire	He avoids the food.
Thomas More is threatened with death by the king.	He accepts the threat as part of God's providence.	Calmed fear; peaceful acceptance	He willingly undergoes death.
Morty Thomas is threatened with death by the king.	He thinks it is unjust because he is innocent.	Anger, indignation	He unwillingly goes to his death.
I feel sleepy.	I must have Lyme disease.	Worry, panic	I see a doctor for bloodwork.
I feel sleepy.	I went to bed too late.	Annoyed	I avoid videos near bedtime.
A person witnesses racism.	I should hurt others until this stops.	Blind rage	Vandalizes businesses
A person witnesses racism.	God can stop this.	Sadness	Prays
Enduring lockdown for months	I can't be happy without friends nearby.	Depression, lethargy	Cries a lot, distracts self with videos
Enduring lockdown for months	I can use this time to improve myself.	Energized excitement	Learns to play guitar

Ultimately, it is our thoughts—about racism, or lock-down, or anything else—that determine the actions or non-actions that stem from our humanity. Thus, Aquinas calls the soul's power of reason and will the "intrinsic" principle of the human act, for an act is human only when it unfolds from deliberate choice—that is, when it is rational and voluntary.

We naturally believe that our judgments are accurate. We cannot second-guess ourselves in everything. But our judgments are accurate only when they reflect the truth of things. Aquinas defines a true statement as one in which the words—whether expressed or unexpressed by the intel-lect—correspond to reality. It is one thing to acknowledge the existence of some disturbing object, such as the pros-pect of losing your job, or some disturbing emotion, such as paralyzing fear. It is another thing to weigh accurately the object's value for your life.

The example of St. Thomas More has already shown us that to develop heroic habits, we should engage our thoughts to know and weigh what we encounter and to moderate our emotional responses accordingly. He was following the teaching of Christ: "Let not your hearts be troubled; believe in God, believe also in me" (Jn 14:1). By faith in God, one's heart can find peace amidst troubles and loss, for faith teaches that through Christ, God prepares everlasting happiness for us in heaven. Hence, thoughts provided by faith give rise to hope. The psalmist, too, moderated his emotions through his faith-imbued thoughts: "Why are you cast down, O my soul, and why are you disqui-eted within me? Hope in God" (Ps 43:5).

Reasoning and Logic

"Come now, let us reason together," God invited Israel through the prophet Isaiah (Is 1:18). That invitation extends to all humanity, for man is a dynamic being: to achieve greatness, one must learn how to fulfill one's end and to be what reality shows one is intended to be. St. John Henry Newman called this fact of life a "law of progress" as well as a "gift" and a "sacred duty": by acquiring knowledge and exercising one's mind, a person advances his nature, makes progress toward his destiny, and experiences living growth. Human reason naturally asks why things are the way they are because we are perfected through a greater knowledge, understanding, and love of the truth. Indeed, it is a sign of maturity that a person thinks for himself and strives to recognize the objective reality of things.

There are two basic aspects of right reasoning: a) thinking the right *way* and b) thinking true *things*. In what follows, I will address both aspects. First, I will discuss how thinking the right way means reasoning well. Leaving aside issues covered in logic textbooks, I will outline the basics of *the process of reasoning* itself. Second, I will discuss how thinking true things includes starting from true premises. In other words, one's mind must have truth as its object from beginning to end. We will see that whereas the habit of logic is a skill that perfects the processes by which the mind works, the habitual knowledge of the truth perfects the mind as such.

Reasoning is not a cherry on top of whipped cream, a nice bonus to life; it is *necessary* to perfect our humanity. Aquinas states, "The soul . . . reaches to the understanding of truth by arguing, with a certain amount of reasoning and movement." Angels communicate wisdom by immediately illuminating each other's intellects, but for humans, it is otherwise. Just as we need to map out new lands to navigate the world, so reasoning is necessary for us to advance from what is better known to what is less known by way of inquiry and discovery. Once our reasoning arrives at truth, then we *understand*—that is, we apprehend intelligible truth, especially the essence of a thing. Aquinas explains, "To reason is to advance from one thing understood to another, so as to know an intelligible truth." Both reasoning and understanding separate us from sub-human animals: we can reason about events and our reactions to them and try to reach the truth of things, whereas they cannot know the truth. Beasts do not even desire the truth, for their world is fenced in by emotions and instincts.

According to Newman, our most natural way of reasoning is concrete. Seen in the farmer who knows that it will rain without exactly being able to explain why, or the mother who is sure that her child has done something wrong despite the child's denial, the ordinary mode of reasoning does not proceed step by step but grasps the import of various phenomena all at once, though a person might not be fully conscious of them. It seems like an instinct, but this sort of reasoning is more than sub-rational intuition: it has been honed by experience, many ponderings, personal character, and other sorts of habit. This natural mode of reasoning is therefore very personal: "an intellectual question may strike two minds very differently, may awaken in them distinct associations . . . and lead them to opposite conclusions."

Adults judge for themselves, by their own lights, on their own principles. Such personal reasoning, of course, is liable to error. The more formal mode of reasoning by logic helps to clarify matters. This sort of reasoning was illustrated in the last chapter, in which we took baby steps to understand the rational soul. We began considering jellyfish, then thought about elephants, and finally we arrived to a higher truth about the human soul. More significant for heroic habits, in Christ, God invites us all to deliberate about the truth. Jesus Christ used logic, deliberation, and holy rhetoric to persuade others of the truth. When the head of a synagogue argues that Jesus should not heal on the Sabbath, Jesus replied, "Does not each of you on the sabbath untie his ox or his ass from the manger, and lead it away to water it? And ought not this woman, a daughter of Abraham whom Satan bound for eighteen years, be loosed from this bond on the sabbath day?" (Lk 13:15–16).

Christ replied with a demonstration that starts from a truth recognized by his interlocutor so that the man could know the truth about things. As Aquinas says, a demonstration is "a syllogism making one to know." Let us consider another example. Christ said to the scribes and Pharisees, "He who is of God hears the words of God; the reason why you do not hear them is that you are not of God" (Jn 8:47). Here, Christ is using a hypothetical syllogism, one that takes the form commonly called *modus tollens*, because it involves denying or taking away (*tollens*) the predicate. There are many, many more instances of Christ's reasoning in the Gospels, but these two may suffice to show that reasoning perfects the mind, that Christ was eminently reasonable, and that Christ employed reasoning so that *we* might be more reasonable by thinking as he does. Contrary to those who hold that "being logical" is problematic for the spiritual life—or, as one might say, for developing the most heroic habits—being logical simply means being reasonable.

Logic produces many useful outcomes: it orders our thinking; it reduces mental chaos; it catalogues our knowledge; it indicates areas of ambiguity; it maps relations among fields of knowledge; it corrects thinking itself; it enables many thinkers to compare their thoughts on the same thing. There are, therefore, significant advantages to logical reasoning.

First, the definite principles and laws of logical thought enable a person to grasp reality on a larger scale, and in a better-ordered system, than what we grasp in our day-to-day thinking. Gregor Mendel's logical thinking helped him develop from being a mere gardener of pea plants to a discoverer of genetics.

Second, just as writing helps codify and correct memory, so logic helps one to analyze his thoughts, and the thoughts of others, so as to avoid serious mistakes.

Third, by ordering the process of thought, logic serves as a sort of reliable key that opens a treasure-house of objective truth available to those who wield it.

Whereas the advantages of logic are less lauded in our day, its limitations are perhaps more familiar. Right logic on its own will no more get us to the truth than a powerful but unguided sports car will get a driver to her destination. Logic, like life itself, needs to start from a right place and be rightly directed toward a right end. As Newman observes, when there is a difficulty in pursuing the truth, the difficulty commonly lies in determining the first principles of our thought, not in the arrangement of logical proofs. This leads us to the second aspect of right reasoning—namely, thinking about the truth.

What Shapes the Mind

When directing a stage production, popular ethicist Jack Marshall says he is often faced with an unpleasant choice: should he call the results of a cast rehearsal "good" when in fact it was a disaster? Perhaps a positive approach could bolster morale and still leave room for constructive criticism. But Jack does not play that way. If it was a dumpster fire, he will say so, for three very important reasons. He writes:

> The first is that if I call what is not good *good*, the performers, or some of them, will begin to believe that what they have given me *is* good, when it is not. This means that they will continue to do what has produced unsatisfactory results.
>
> The second is that if they know they weren't good, they will either think that their leader and manager doesn't know what good is, thus costing him their trust, or they will realize I am lying to them, which undermines their trust as well.
>
> The third reason is that it's *true*.

Let's focus on the last reason. Although the truth might sting, it is good for a person to know it. We grasp this, at least intuitively, even when it might be inconvenient. St. John Paul II explained, "People cannot be genuinely indifferent to the question of whether what they know is true or not. If they discover that it is false, they reject it; but if they can establish its truth, they feel themselves rewarded." As St. Augustine shrewdly observed, "I have met many who wanted to deceive, but none who wanted to be deceived."

Truth perfects the mind by shaping it and conforming it to reality. The chief perfective habits related to possessing the truth are called "intellectual virtues." *Science*, in Aquinas's terminology, is the habit by which one possesses certain knowledge. Knowledge comes from a direct apprehension of the truth joined to an accurate judgment about it, in which case our mind corresponds to reality, as noted. *Understanding* is the intellect's habit of grasping the principles that undergird the essence of a thing: when you truly understand a thing, you penetrate to the core of its nature. *Wisdom* is the habit of intellectually seeing the first principles of being; it judges all knowable things and sets them in order in light of the highest causes. *Art* is the habit that perfects reason's guidance of one's power to shape the exterior world in accord with the true, the good, and the beautiful, whether through mechanical works such as engineering or through the finer arts of music, sculpture, painting, and so on. Finally, there is *prudence*, which is the habit of the intellect as applied to one's character so that a person shapes himself into the best human he can be by doing the right things at the right time for the right reasons.

Faith in Christ is the chief virtue of the mind. Whereas the other intellectual virtues on their own can remain on the cognitive level, living faith—that is, faith enlivened by charity—sets a person free for greater things and thereby contributes to a person's overall perfection. Less solid than knowledge, *opinion* is a mere conjecture we hold about something, but without certitude: we lean to one side of things, while being concerned about the other side. A person with an *opinion* that Christ is God is less settled than a person who has a strong, settled *belief* of the same. Hence, habits of opinion do not perfect the mind.

Higher principles held by the mind are more general, speculative, and related to the natures of things: these should guide the lower principles, including the principles of action. In the final sections of this chapter, I will offer two examples of how principles of action operate concretely. Here, I will anticipate that exposition a bit. An abstract principle is called a *maxim*. A speculative maxim could be "All people desire to know the truth." A practical maxim could be "It is good to love one's country." More concrete principles for action, opinions shared by a particular group, which might be applicable only to a particular context, are called *endoxa* (singular: *endoxon*); for example, "Voting is a sign of love of one's country." Both maxims and endoxa might be inculcated in us from childhood. Often, we advert to them without full awareness. More encompassing, but even less present to consciousness, is what Newman called a "habit of *viewing*" and a "stand-point." It underlies all mental habituation, indeed, all human habituation, and therefore deserves a careful explanation.

The mind needs some principle to organize the myriad impressions it receives: colors, angles and curves, sounds like squeals and hums, words we read or hear, as well as *internal* reactions such as emotions, non-deliberative estimations, memories, and so on. When receiving these objects, the mind throws them into a system, uniting and stamping them with one form. A child, for example, looks upon the world with her childish view—all things interpreted in light of her petty concerns, her mental world dominated by thoughts of momma and dada, and what fragments of knowledge she has acquired. In contrast, a politician tends to frame what he encounters in light of his concern for his public image, how voters might respond, what policies could be spun out in response, and so on. This mental method is an acquired habit that feels so natural, and operates so spontaneously, that only with attention is a person aware of it. Newman argues that "though it is no easy matter to view things correctly, nevertheless the busy mind will ever be viewing. We cannot do without a view, and we put up with an illusion when we cannot get a truth." Here, Newman seems to have anticipated the concept of *weltanschauung* (worldview) as explained by Heidegger: "a self-realized, productive as well as conscious way of apprehending and interpreting the universe of beings." A worldview, then, is like an architectonic background program in a computer to which a front-end user rarely attends.

The psychology of cognitive therapy recognizes a similar phenomenon, which it calls mental schemas. As explained by Jeffrey E. Young and his colleagues, a schema is *a broad pervasive organizing principle that helps individuals to explain their experiences, to mediate perception, and to guide their responses.* An artistic schema could help a person paint a sunset, or a skeptical philosophical schema might lead a person to doubt the truth of every claim he encounters. Significantly, a schema is "comprised of memories, emotions, cognitions, and bodily sensations, regarding oneself and one's relationships with others, [typically] developed during childhood or adolescence, [but] elaborated throughout one's lifetime." It seems that a schema can exist on the level of thought, in which case it would include the levels operative in mental habituation—general principles, maxims, and endoxa—but it has a top-down overflow into the lower powers and creates a more or less unitary principle by which experience is organized, interpreted, and thus felt in the emotions and intuited by the estimative sense.

Schemas can also exist on the subconscious level as intertwined with estimative judgments and emotional reactions, coordinated with memories and various pictures in the imagination. Trauma can create a schema by which a person responds to similar situations with patterned reactions of intense sadness, shame, fear, or anger. In such cases, one's interpretation of a situation feels right, for persons "regard schemas as *a priori* truths, and thus the schemas influence the processing of later experiences. They play a major role in how patients think, feel, act, and relate to others." The following examples illustrate how action is proof that that schemas—with accompanying mental habits—are truly embedded within us. In action, thoughts move from a mere notional existence within the mind to being "realized" in the world: they take flesh in one's life.

Mental Habits and Schemas of Falsehood

A mental habit does not come about by adding one random thought to another. An aggregate of news flashes will no more shape the mind into a solid character and distinctive cast of thought any more than hearing a pop song in a shopping mall will transform a person into a musician. Snippets of information uncritically received can inculcate a mental attitude and emotional floor that constrain further action, but without active and personal engagement with thought, a person will not come to have any firm belief. The habits of knowledge and understanding are slowly built up in the soul as reason proceeds baby step by baby step, accepting one principle after another, until a person develops a mental schema or framework that provides unity and order to these various thoughts and, going beyond a mere notional existence, realizes and actualizes them in his life. Because not all principles are true, not all mental habits are equally good.

To illustrate two extreme types of mental habituation, I shall here discuss the radical reconditioning depicted in George Orwell's dystopian novel *Nineteen Eighty-Four*, and in the next section, the conversion of St. John Henry Newman. As we shall see, these processes are almost inverted mirrors of one another.

Orwell's description of mental habituation in his novel *Nineteen Eighty-Four* provides a model for understanding how anyone adopts falsehood in one way or another. The plot is linear. After having experienced some amount of mental freedom from the tyranny of fake news—which he helped to create—and a grey world of lies, the main character Winston Smith is snatched up by government police and taken to a facility called the "Ministry of Love." Winston's lover, Julia, had believed that the mind was free, no matter what happened to one's body. Orwell shows to the contrary how functionaries expertly used torture to establish new *habits of thought* in their victim. Their explicit purpose was to move Winston from learning their lessons, to understanding them, then to interiorizing and accepting them. Only then could he be "reintegrated" with society.

The first phase of the new learning was to use threat and torture to inculcate within him a bestial fear of their power. "How many times he had been beaten, how long the beatings had continued, he could not remember. Always there were five or six men in black uniforms at him simultaneously. . . . There were times when he rolled about the floor, as shameless as an animal, writhing his body this way and that in an endless, hopeless effort to dodge the kicks, and simply inviting more and yet more kicks, in his ribs, in his belly, on his elbows, on his shins, in his groin, in his testicles, on the bone at the base of his spine."

The sign of their success was that in response to the mere *threat* of the painful stimulus, he was willing to forsake the truth: "There were times when his nerve so forsook him that he began shouting for mercy even before the beating began, when the mere sight of a fist drawn back for a blow was enough to make him pour forth a confession of real and imaginary crimes."

The second phase was to break down Winston's power of reasoning so that he would accept whatever claims they fed him.

His questioners now were not ruffians in black uniforms but Party intellectuals, little rotund men. . . .
They slapped his face, wrung his ears, pulled his hair,
made him stand on one leg, refused him leave to uri-
nate, shone glaring lights in his face until his eyes ran
with water; but *the aim of this was simply to humili-
ate him and destroy his power of arguing and reasoning.*
Their real weapon was the merciless questioning that
went on and on, hour after hour, tripping him up,
laying traps for him, twisting everything that he said,
convicting him at every step of lies and self-contradic-
tion until he began weeping as much from shame as
from nervous fatigue.(emphasis added)

The sign of the success was that he was willing to confess
even absurdities. "In the end the nagging voices broke him
down more completely than the boots and fists of the guards.
He became simply a mouth that uttered, a hand that signed,
whatever was demanded of him. His sole concern was to
find out what they wanted him to confess, and then confess
it quickly, before the bullying started anew. . . . He confessed
that he had murdered his wife, although he knew, and his
questioners must have known, that his wife was still alive."

The last phase was to habituate Winston's mind to accept
a series of thoughts that ranged from abstract principles to
very specific claims, as well as a general way of "thinking with
the Party." They were successful in this too. The most general
principle furrowed into his mind was that anything could be
true if the Party said it. Thus, Winston came to believe that
two and two equals five. He also accepted certain maxims

that served to guide thought and action: FREEDOM IS
SLAVERY, IGNORANCE IS STRENGTH, and GOD IS
POWER.

In order to actualize the maxim "IGNORANCE IS
STRENGTH," one must realize that in a concrete situation,
"to consider this sort of thought would lead to non-igno-
rance"; that is, thinking might lead to knowledge, which,
in that worldview, would be weakness. Again, the maxim
"FREEDOM IS SLAVERY," and its correlate "SLAVERY IS
FREEDOM," call for an endoxon such as "to have freedom
of thought would be slavery; true freedom means slavery of
my thoughts to the Party." To stamp the maxims and endoxa
of the Party into his mind, Winston therefore forced himself
to overcome his mental repugnance at blatant absurdity. He
trained his mind to reject any dangerous thought automatically, instantaneously, and instinctively. The Party called this
deeply ingrained habit *crimestop*.

The Party built upon the automatic cognitive thoughts
with which it habituated Winston, introducing a new
schema into Winston. His torturers knew that to change his
behavior, they needed to habituate his deepest fear impulses,
his instinctual responses to danger and potential reward,
his imagination of future tortures, his memory of a lover,
as well as various levels of conscious thoughts. Thus, Winston's deep habituation in favor of the Party was manifested
at end of the novel when, without exterior compulsion, he
chose indifference toward Julia, the lover he had betrayed
under torture. But his transformation was complete when
he turned from her, was emotionally moved by propaganda,

and shed a couple of tears out of a genuine feeling of love for Big Brother.

The psychologist Albert Ellis notes that once generated, the consequences of one habit loop can become antecedents to another habit loop, linking them all in a chain that reinforces an all-encompassing habit. Winston's experiences can thus be summarized in the following chart.

	Habit loop 1	Habit loop 2	Habit loop 3	Habit loop 4
Antecedent	Torture			
Behavior	Physiological, emotional terror			
Consequent/ Antecedent 2	Thought: torture might return	Thought: torture might return		
Behavior		Terror in the imagination, memory, emotions		
Consequent/ Antecedent 3		Declare lies	Declare lies	
Behavior			Feeling of calm	
Consequent/ Antecedent 4			Accept lies	Accept lies
Behavior				Love Big Brother
Consequent				Reintegration with the Party

Orwell's narrative shows the devastating successes that may be wrought by deep habituation to falsehood and evil.

Techniques and technologies that have developed since the 1940s reinforce Orwell's grim conclusion.

Mental Habits and Schemas of the Truth

On the night of October 8, 1845, Dominic Barberi, a priest of the Passionist Congregation, endured five hours of driving rain while traveling. He arrived completely exhausted at Littlemore, a hamlet only a few miles from Oxford, which served as a refuge and retreat for John Henry Newman. As Barberi was drying himself before a fire, Newman knelt down and told the Italian missionary that he would not move from there until he was blessed and received into the Catholic Church. Newman proceeded to make his confession through much of the night. After a break, he completed his confession the next day and received absolution. Father Barberi later wrote, "What a spectacle it was for me to see Newman at my feet! All that I have suffered since I left Italy has been well compensated by this event. I hope the effects of such a conversion may be great." Newman's humble act, his self-surrender, was the culmination of many years of inquiry and search for divine truth. Hardly any example of positive habituation could be more contrary to Winston's "re-education" in Orwell's *Nineteen Eighty-Four*.

St. John Henry Newman's assent to Catholicism, along with its moral maxims and schema of faith, if one can put it that way, was by no means a foregone conclusion. As a young Anglican clergyman, Newman boldly declared, "I do not suppose that any of us are likely to fall away to Popery. It is not in the way for churchmen to depart from their excellent forms and worship to the corruptions of the Romish Church. . . . Sober churchmen are in no danger from the Pope." In 1840, five years before his conversion, Newman had written that he must "keep aloof" from the Catholic Church until he saw in it "more straightforwardness, truth, and openness, more of severe obedience to God's least commandments . . . less of a political, scheming, grasping spirit, less of intrigue, less that looks hollow and superficial . . . less intimacy with the revolutionary spirit of the day." He claimed that the Roman Church in England was everywhere associated with "the spirit of rebellion, the lust of change, the unthankfulness of the irreligious, and the enviousness of the needy." Not long after, Newman's judgment of the Catholic Church would entirely change.

So drastic and pervasive was the transformation that many years later, Charles Kingsley would challenge Newman's sincerity and even his commitment to honest dealings. Newman's reply revealed the reasons behind his conversion in a text he entitled *Apologia Pro Vita Sua* (Explanation/ Defense of His Life). That text quotes a letter he had written nearly a year before his conversion in which he said, "My one paramount reason for contemplating a change is my deep, unvarying conviction that our [Anglican] Church is in schism, and that my salvation depends on my joining the Church of Rome." He was well aware that his conversion might distress some of his friends and followers, and even unsettle their confidence in the reality of truth and falsehood. After all, if he had been so strong against Rome before on the grounds of truth, how could he now enter into her embrace? He responded, "It should be considered whether such change is not *necessary*, if truth be a real objective thing, and be made to confront a person who has been brought up in a system *short* of truth. Surely the *continuance* of a person, who wishes to go right, in a wrong system, and not his *giving it up*, would be that which militated against the objectiveness of Truth."

Anticipating claims of base motivation, Newman clarified that he would give up one system for another not out of resentment or disgust with Anglicans, nor from any existing sympathies for Catholics, nor for any plots to hatch as a Catholic. Unlike Winston Smith's forced "love" for Big Brother, Newman was not coerced to enter the Church. He became Catholic not to avoid some terrible punishment, nor to gain any worldly reward. In becoming Catholic, he gave up much that he loved and prized and could have retained as an Anglican. But he made the sacrifice because he loved honesty better than honor and Truth better than dear friends.

By habituating himself to seeking the truth wherever he might find it, and in holding fast to it once found, Newman opened himself to the possibility of conversion whereby he would replace one set of mental habits with another. He recognized that for the Catholic Church, "all true conversion must begin with the first springs of thought." He interpreted Christ's injunction "you must be born again" to mean "your whole nature must be re-born, your passions, and your affections, and your aims, and your conscience, and your will, must all be bathed in a new element, and reconsecrated to your Maker,—and, the last not the least, your intellect." Ultimately, Newman suffered much to embrace the Truth out of a free, loving, and "strict obedience to the light which had already been granted [him]." Despite heartache, his was the path of homecoming.

The writings of the Church Fathers were decisive "triggers" for Newman's new thought. His epoch-making *Essay on the Development of Christian Doctrine*, completed near the time of his conversion, accounts for doctrinal, ecclesial, and personal development. Newman's development entailed a new faith that the Catholic Church is the one true Church founded by Jesus Christ, the one true home for the soul, and that it speaks infallibly in certain carefully defined situations. Unlike Winston Smith, who violated his mind's integrity by believing that 2 + 2 = 5, Newman saw that a Catholic, layman or priest, is not indifferent to the Church's teaching, nor will accept anything a prelate might happen to teach, for Catholic faith does not destroy the intellect. Rather, as Newman detailed in his *Letter to the Duke of Norfolk* (1874), as Catholics hold fast to their faith as infallibly taught by the Church, such fidelity is strengthened, not weakened, through personal inquiry.

Unless a person is at liberty to investigate according to the peculiarities of his own knowledge and understanding, Newman argued, one is not free to investigate at all and the truth may not be found. "It is the very law of the human mind," he said, "in its inquiry after and acquisition of truth to make its advances by a process which consists of many stages, and is circuitous. There are no short cuts to knowledge." Just as a train cannot climb straight up a mountain, and just as a sailboat cannot make a line to port without tacking, so it is with acquiring truth: the mind must have its "elbow room," as it were, to exercise itself as it strives to understand something truly. To allow for this seemingly haphazard process, the only process by which one's mind becomes fully habituated to reality as to something co-natural to it is to have confidence in the truth, "a great and firm belief in the sovereignty of Truth. Error may flourish for a time, but Truth will prevail in the end. The only effect of error ultimately is to promote Truth."

After many debates, many restless nights of pondering, much study of Greek and Latin authors, many attempts to reconcile the religion of his youth with the truth as he could see it, after much writing, much controversy, many questions, and difficult answers, Newman was convinced that he had found the truth. Two days before he converted to Catholicism, Newman made a retraction of anti-Catholic statements; for the rest of his life, he submitted his writings to Church authorities to ensure their conformity with the teaching of Christ promulgated and taught by the Catholic Church. In these ways, Newman showed that he had fully adopted the Catholic worldview which informed not only his expressions but also his thoughts and his very heart. His conversion, he said, "was like coming into port after a rough sea." Many years after the fact, Newman reported, "I have had no variations to record, and have had no anxiety of heart whatever. I have been in perfect peace and contentment. . . . Ten thousand difficulties do not make one doubt."

On the surface, there seem to be noteworthy similarities between Winston's habituation to Party thinking in Orwell's *Nineteen Eighty-Four* and John Henry Newman's conversion to Catholicism. Both endured pain in a process which made their thoughts, indeed their whole persons, docile to a great human authority and its representatives. A deeper examination, however, shows how intensely different were the object, process, and outcomes of their respective habituations. No priest kicked Newman to convince his mind, no bishop browbeat him into submission. But brute force and trickery were the means by which Winston was conditioned. It was the anguish of pain and terror that forced Winston to open his mind to accept general principles of the Party, whereas Newman accepted the authority of the pope as an exercise of his spiritual freedom. Winston was led by a desire to save his life, whereas Newman meant to save his soul. Winston had to teach himself to accept absurdities that contradicted his memories and what he had previously known, whereas Newman's understanding and knowledge organically developed from truth to truth. Winston came to accept that the Party was always right, even when it contradicted itself, but Newman came to see that the pope is infallible only when universally teaching on faith and morals, and never in contradiction with Church tradition. Winston twisted his faculties to receive maxims such as "IGNORANCE IS STRENGTH," whereas Newman held "Truth will prevail." Winston dully applied maxims of the Party and ceased to love, whereas Newman never ceased to love even when life called for a parting of friends.

In sum, Winston's transformation was a diminishment of his person, as he accepted lies, hate, and evil for the sake of self-preservation, but Newman's conversion dignified and perfected him, since he freely chose to live in accord with reality, even when it meant embracing the cross. Through his conversion, Newman learned to think with the Church, which was much more than adopting a mental worldview that was positively adaptive by helping him meet his goals. It was putting on the mind of Christ and living in accord with the truth. The mechanical habit loop might well represent the process by which Winston was habituated to become a "Party man," but it can only dimly model how Newman was transformed, not by a human invention directed toward power politics, but by a deeper relation with God, who is Truth itself.

Here, I can only hint at the extraordinarily important role of contemplation and the Gifts of the Holy Spirit. They perfect the mind by making it docile to the direct movements of God. The example of St. John Henry Newman, and all the heroes of faith, shows us that when we contemplate the truth and wisdom of God, the Holy Spirit will make great changes within us. As Cornelius à Lapide said, "The thought of wisdom leads to wisdom, for whoever thinks about a thing often comes to love it, and when Wisdom is loved, it seeks out the lover and communicates itself to him."

CHAPTER 5

HEROIC HABITS

Now that we have been together for four chapters, I need to face the music. I began this book about heroic habits with the example of St. Thomas Aquinas. For many readers, it might seem odd that I proposed *him* as an example of heroic habits. After all, he is best known for his extraordinary literary productions. He was a nerd's nerd: a hero for the bookish type, perhaps, but how heroic is that? Since I am discussing "heroic" habits, why not a more obviously heroic figure? Among the saints, we find St. Damien de Veuster and his patient labors among the lepers of Molokai, St. Francis Xavier on his missionary journeys to India, China, and Japan, or St. Catherine of Siena with her work in reconciling Christendom while performing miracles and exorcisms.

Furthermore, some might say that saints seem too distant from average readers, so why not discuss modern superheroes? Perhaps I could take a hint from a book series called *DC Super Heroes Character Education*. It includes titles such as "Superman is a Good Citizen," "The Flash is Caring," and "Wonder Woman is Respectful." Odd, though: none of the children's books focus on what is most obvious about superheroes—namely, their fighting abilities. It is as if the "character education" creators are worried that children might become violent. Satires of superhero movies show how easy it would be for superheroes to use their powers for evil. Once we realize this, the surprising thing is not that Superman and gang do good but that they don't do evil. Their real heroism lies not in raw force honed through a training montage. Heroism is more than mere combat readiness. As this chapter will show, and as Aquinas shows us, the greatest excellence is excellence of character.

Heroism and Power

The idea of heroism has inspired action for millennia. The epic Greek poet Hesiod described heroes as a "race of godlike men . . . called demigods." Exemplary were the men of the *Iliad*, the *Odyssey*, and the *Aeneid*: Achilles, Odysseus, Hector, Aeneas, and lesser compatriots. Heroes were seen as having a "liminal nature," existing on the margins between gods and men—subjected to mortal passions and the changes of necessity but rising above them as the slopes of Mount Olympus rise above the hills. Heroes were not worshipped as gods, but their tombs were visited, their deeds were extolled, and hallowed rites were offered in their names. Aristotle, following Hesiod and Homer, describes a hero as a person who exists between the brutes and the gods. A beastlike person is *beneath* human nature by defect, whereas a hero is *above* human nature by excess of excellence and exists in a "godlike state." Hence, contrary to brutishness is "superhuman excellence, something heroic and divine." Both brutish men and heroes are rare.

When the sun had already set on the "age of heroes," Herodotus, the first historian of the West, could still identify true heroism. Above all were the Greeks who fought against the Persian king Xerxes. Herodotus praises the warriors of Athens for their foresight and naval victories: "They chose that Hellas should survive in freedom; and after rousing to that cause all other Greeks who had not capitulated to Xerxes, they repelled the King with the help of the gods." For this reason, he calls the Athenians "the saviors of Greece." Better known are the three hundred Spartan warriors who joined their ruler Leonidas to hold back the Persian hordes in the battle of Thermopylae. The barbarian forces outnumbered the Spartans 750 to 1—so many that when their arrows flew, the sun was blocked from sight. Herodotus emphasizes that the Greeks fought better because they were more disciplined, they interiorized good laws within themselves, and they were not slaves: "The Greeks make it clear to everyone, and especially to the King himself, that although there were many in his army, there were few real men."

Can the modern world produce heroes like the ancient Athenians and Spartans? Recall that here we are not interested in one-off actions that achieve spectacular results. We are looking for heroic *habits*: stable qualities of the soul that make a person great and thereby incline us toward greatness throughout our lives.

To the modern mind, heroic habits and greatness get the cold shoulder: moral goodness seems better represented by kindness, care for the earth, and pleasant emotions. Across a great chasm stand dignified strength, nobility, and an unwillingness to compromise with falsehood. The adage of

Lord Acton summarizes present sentiments: "Power tends to corrupt and absolute power corrupts absolutely." This well-known statement is followed by the lesser-known lines "Great men are almost always bad men, even when they exercise influence and not authority: still more when you superadd the tendency or the certainty of corruption by authority." Acton made his observation about power as a historian considering the effects of nearly unlimited papal and kingly rule. The record of Henry VIII, the Borgia family, and many others make his position plausible. The greatest evils are often committed by the most powerful men, and many men were good when powerless but became evil when they ascended to the throne. Hence, twinkly-eyed nuns and chubby, smiling old men can be accepted as "heroes," but warriors do not have much of a chance unless they are anti-heroes with compromising flaws, or soldiers used as tokens for political purposes.

Alexander the Great seems to exemplify Acton's adage. Undoubtedly, Alexander was one of the world's greatest warriors and tacticians. How else could he defeat armies from Greece, Egypt, Persia, Babylon, and India? But he was more than a successful killer. Arrian describes how Alexander possessed a pronounced nobility of soul, manifested in a hundred ways: Alexander piously honored the gods wherever he went; he took up weapons from the tombs in Troy and honored the heroes whom he would imitate. He cared about his soldiers: he knew their names, spoke with them, and listened to their accounts of battle. He chose to honor Darius's beautiful wife rather than violate her after capturing her in battle. When warned that his medicine was poisoned, he boldly drank the liquid in order to show his friendship with the doctor who had prepared it. When his generals argued about assaulting a seemingly-impregnable city, Alexander said that for the sake of greatness, "the harder the conquest, the more it should be attempted." He once left a tribe free from his dominion because they were self-governed and not imbued with a slave morality. And when he and his men were dying from thirst while traversing a desert, he refused to drink a cup of water when they could have none.

Simultaneously, the precious metal of Alexander's character was mixed with baser stuff. Arrian describes Alexander's impetuosity, his self-indulgence, his rare but real cruelty, and the fact that he was mastered by his passion for battle and lust for glory. It seems that these faults grew as his power grew. Eventually, Alexander imitated the Persian tyrants he had conquered. He certainly was "a man who became so great and attained such a peak of human success as the undisputed king of both continents whose name reached every land," but, the historian makes clear, Alexander would have been greater had his virtue been more perfect.

Does Alexander's example prove that power corrupts? Before conceding the point, we should note that Acton said power *tends* to corrupt. It would be entirely erroneous to say that power in itself corrupts, or is a corruption. Thomas Aquinas explains that power is the ability to act, to be a cause. The higher a being is, the more it has power, for "power is proportionate to the being of which it is a power . . . power flows from the essence of a thing." Because God's being is perfect, there is no potential within him. He is perfectly actual, and his power does not develop; it cannot increase.

He is all-powerful: he can do all things that are possible in themselves. He is the cause and source of all power, transcending all created power, empowering whatever is weak, sustaining all things in their being. God's very essence shows that power is, in itself, something positive.

From the perspective of creatures, all goods can be divided into three categories: goods exterior to ourselves, goods of the body, and goods of the soul. Because the natural form of a created thing is its soul, the greater its soul, the greater is its power. Whatever exists has the power *to be*; plant life is a greater power than mere existence; animal life is above that of plants; and the intellect and will are still higher powers. A tree cannot grow without some interior power that causes it to thrust its roots further into the ground and to stretch out its branches and to bear forth leaves and fruit. An animal cannot move itself without an interior power that gives it life and energy and sentience. A dead fish will float downstream, but only a living, powerful fish can swim against the current. Humans, too, need power in order to think and decide, to move ourselves to our highest good. The coach potato squanders his physical power, and if a gym rat does not exercise his mind, he limits his mental powers. All of this created power comes ultimately from God's power: "In short, nothing in the world lacks the almighty power of God to support and to surround it, for that which completely lacks power has neither existence, nor individuality, nor even a place in the world."

Creatures can possess another basic source of power—namely, a form added to their souls. Aquinas calls these added forms "habits." Habits perfect particular powers, enabling them to reach a higher perfection than when they exist in their relatively less formed, less organized state. Some habits are lower-level skills with limited application because they focus on limited goods: "Where there is too much of them, they must either do harm, or at any rate be of no use." Expertise in manipulating spreadsheets will not win friends and influence people outside of the office; encyclopedic knowledge of Anime does not confer fluency in Japanese; excellence in the videogame Guitar Hero neither makes one a guitarist nor a hero. Small skills produce small results. In contrast, "every good of the soul, the greater it is, is also of greater use." Hence, habits that intensify one's love of the highest truths, and which direct one's soul to the highest goods, are nobler and more useful.

Habits that improve higher faculties and strengthen the spiritual soul offer the greatest boosts of power. Often, it is thought that being "virtuous" is equivalent to "following the rules." But virtue is more than an external change of behavior; it is a stable habit that denotes goodness of character, a goodness that entails the perfection of power. The etymology of the word *virtue* is revelatory. "Virtue" comes from the Latin *virtus*, which means "power." A virtue is the result of the right exercise of a power and, therefore, its more perfect state—similar to how physical strength is the result of right physical exercise of one's muscles. A virtue, as a resting state of increased strength aimed in the right direction, is also a latent power to perform a right action in the future. A person who perfects his power to choose for the sake of the good possesses the virtue of justice, which is an interior power that enables him to make just decisions in the future with ease, skill, quickness, and joy; a person who perfects his power to think in practical terms possesses the virtue/power of prudence; a person who perfects his aggressive, assertive desires, possesses courage; and a person who perfects his lower desires for pleasure enjoys the power of temperance. An overall virtuous person is one who has increased his overall personal power by honing and perfecting his various individual powers in coordination with one another through the integrating power of right reason.

Goodness, then, is the perfection of a thing, and perfection is an increase of power. Good and evil are not co-principles in the universe. Good is more powerful than evil. Evil is always a corruption of the good, a diminishment, a lacking, an emptiness. Consequently, actuality, virtue, nature, goodness, and reasonableness go together with power. The ancient Christian writer called Dionysius makes this very clear: "Evil, *qua* evil, never produces being or birth. All it can do by itself is in a limited fashion to debase and to destroy the substance of things. . . . Evil therefore in itself has neither being, goodness, the capacity to beget, nor the ability to create things which have being and goodness."

It follows that power in itself does not corrupt; it cannot corrupt: evil corrupts, and all corruption is evil. Power is evil when it is directed to the wrong end, when it is used in the wrong way, or when it is corrupted in some other manner. In itself, power is good, and the greatest greatness is greatness of soul; the highest excellence is heroism of habits.

Credited as the tutor of Alexander the Great, Aristotle grasped the nature of greatness by explaining that heroism is mediated through a meta-habit, which he called *megalopsychia*, literally, "greatness of soul." Greatness of soul is "a sort of crown of the virtues, for it makes them greater, and it is not found without them." By greatness of soul, a person strives to do eminent and beautiful things: eminent because they rise above the measure of ordinary virtue and beautiful because their prominence is well-proportioned in an excellent way and uncompromised by the ugliness of a reductive and crass efficiency. One can define a heroic habit as "a disposition to perform splendid actions on a huge scale and in a grand manner." The greater the habit one possesses within one's soul, the more it extends in the world as well as in the soul, making a person's actions and his very person heroic. Accordingly, Arrian described Alexander of Macedon not merely as a great warrior, or a great tactician, but as a great *man*.

Here, we may return to Lord Acton's claim that power tends to corrupt. We have seen that excellence ≅ greatness ≅ heroism ≅ extraordinary virtue ≅ perfected and directed power. An argument could be made that Alexander was not truly morally great. He lacked an all-around heroism of habit. It is hardly deniable that ancient heroes would have been more heroic had they possessed virtue in every way in addition to whatever heroic qualities they did have. The cause of Alexander's corruption was that he lacked complete virtue—that is, the power to direct his soul aright. A moral disorder existed in his heart before he conquered the world, and power acted upon his disorder as sugar acts upon fat cells, feeding them and helping them spread. Acton correctly argues that political power must indeed be regulated. This is less because of power in itself and more because *sin* corrupts the individual and inclines the powerful to use power poorly, much as our disordered eating habits incline us to eat too much sugar. It follows that the greatest greatness, and most important factor for heroic habits, is the interior reality of perfected virtue whereby we can use goods of the world most effectively.

Philosopher Howard Curzer argues that heroism belongs to more than world-conquering paladins. Great actions can be either a) ordinary virtuous actions performed under extremely trying conditions or b) extremely virtuous actions performed under ordinary circumstances. The key is virtue, which means power directed toward the right end, used rightly. Curzer's interpretation fits remarkably well with the Catholic understanding of virtue, and it brings us back to the issue that began this chapter. Some saints manifest heroic habits in ordinary circumstances: we might think of St. Teresa of Calcutta and her care for the poorest of the poor, or St. Thérèse of Lisieux, whose writings about the "Little Way" to heaven have inspired millions. Other saints manifest heroic habits in extraordinarily difficult circumstances, as when the martyrs St. Lawrence and St. Ignatius of Antioch witnessed to the faith despite horrendous torture. Underlying both of these kinds of heroic habits is their very essence: not so much the circumstances in which an action is performed but the intensity and the motive for which one acts. There is a third kind of a heroic action that Curzer overlooked—namely, to perform extraordinarily virtuous deeds under extraordinarily trying circumstances. Such was seen in the lives of such saints as Francis Xavier and Damien of Molokai.

Thomas says that the greatest, most splendid actions are above all perfect works of virtue. A truly great-souled person performs his great acts with humility, which make his habits even more heroic, for he realizes that all greatness comes from God, especially the gifts of grace that surpass natural human power even more than human nature surpasses that of a jellyfish. Here, we find the example of Jesus Christ, who attested, "Greater love has no man than this, that he lay down his life for his friends" (Jn 15:13). Christ's greatness went beyond this. His love was so heroic that he laid down his life not only for his friends but also for his enemies so that he might win them over to be friends (see Rom 5:8). At the same time, as God, Christ was simultaneously all-powerful and all-good. Heroic habits, therefore, are most heroic when they are most Christlike.

Principles of Heroic Habits

Christ is the "primordial exemplar" of all goodness, and especially of all spiritual graces with which spiritual creatures are illuminated. Hence, Christ "possesses exemplarily in himself the splendors of all the saints." Reciprocally, the saints serve as examples of acquiring and developing Christlike habits because of their unity in Christ. Through their diverse individuality, which leads to a splendorous variety in natural habits, in degrees of charity, and in expressions of infused virtues and Gifts of the Holy Spirit, the saints exemplify the many different ways in which heroic habits may come to full flourishing. On account of the imperfection of the current state of the world, "the clarity of the saints is hidden from us in this life, just as is the darkness of the wicked." Nevertheless, even now, God works so that these paragons of virtue can shine like "cities on a hill" and be seen by many so that they may guide us to our homeland in heaven (see Mt 5:14).

St. Anthony Mary Claret had a particular love for the saints. In his autobiography, he described how the saints powerfully intensified his own good habits, especially the abiding desire he had to be another apostle:

> I frequently read the lives of those saints who were distinguished for their zeal in saving souls, and I felt the good effect of it. . . . In the course of meditating on the lives and works of these saints, I used to feel such a burning within me that I couldn't sit still. I had to get up and run from one place to another, preaching continually. I can't describe what I felt inside me. Nothing tired me; I wasn't terrified at the awful calumnies being leveled against me, or afraid of the greatest persecutions. Everything was sweet to me, as long as I could win souls for Jesus Christ and heaven and save them from hell.

St. Anthony then related how female saints impressed him with their lives even more than the male saints, deeply moving him to greater heroism. The result was that he became like an intinerant Padre Pio in the late 1800s in Spain. He performed miracles of healing and of knowing consciences; he had visions of the Blessed Virgin and of future events; he traveled thousands of miles on foot to preach, and he endured cold and hunger and attempts on his life, all of which only intensified his heroic habits.

To grasp the essence of heroic habits, we can hardly find any better source than the classic treatise *On the Beatification and Canonization of the Servants of God* written between 1734 and 1738 by Prospero Lambertini, later Pope Benedict XIV. There he describes in sparkling detail that what makes a person a saint is precisely heroic virtue. Although any person close to God possesses the good habits of virtue, yet not every person reaches the all-encompassing high degree of excellence in habits recognized by canonization. Following Aquinas, Lambertini argues that anyone can have some sort of virtue, such as fortitude and patience. These individual habits can even rise to the level of heroism in a narrow field, as when Napoleon consistently manifested extraordinary courage on the battlefield throughout his life. However, only faith and charity provide the principles by which habits can be integrated with one another, and exist in a harmonious union by being directed to the supreme ultimate end—namely, God himself.

Heroic habits within a Christian come from God and lead to God. Lambertini therefore equates heroic habits with "divine and theological" virtue "which God infuses into our minds, beyond all the requirements of nature, with a view to some end or object above nature." With that sort of virtue, a person "very far surpasses the goodness of other just persons, who aspire more lethargically after Christian perfection." He notes that a person might perform once or twice an *act* that is heroic—such as saving a person from a burning building or witnessing to the truth amid persecution on the job. But to manifest a heroic *habit* requires the individual to have persevered in a high level of virtue in a continued way of life, uninterrupted by frequent falls into grave sin, with purity of heart and a firm and intense love of God above all things: "this way of life, pursued uniformly and invariably for a long time, far surpasses the condition of human nature left to itself." Indeed, "it approaches the Divine Nature, and therefore of itself suffices for evangelical heroicity, because it of itself constitutes a man perfect after the manner that our Father in heaven is perfect." God is not great merely in some *act* he performs, such as creation; rather, he is great in his own personal being. Similarly, a person who possesses all of the virtues united to one another in a superlative degree is a heroic person.

Sanctifying grace is a "certain habitude" which serves as a principle and root of all heroic habits. By sanctifying grace, which is received in the sacrament of Baptism, intensified in the Holy Eucharist, and restored in confession, a quality is added to the soul which lets us habitually participate in divine perfection even in this life. When we develop habits by our own power and effort, they feel like "second nature," for they make actions that flow from them feel natural— that is, easy, skillful, speedy, and resulting in joy. Nevertheless, our human-powered habits will always be imperfect, intertwined with sin, and limited to this world. Suppose a person loses her sight in a terrible acid attack. Dark craters are in her face where her eyes once beamed. Therapy might help her develop her senses of touch and hearing so that she can navigate the world with a cane. But her habitual blindness cannot be healed unless the power of sight is restored, and no exercise can do this. In a similar way, without grace, a person's soul cannot be healed of its aversion from the light of God's truth and the warmth of God's goodness. Following St. Augustine, St. Thomas recalls Christ's healing of the man born blind, saying that it symbolizes our need for the enlightenment of baptism in order to receive spiritual sight. In Aquinas's formulation, grace presupposes nature, grace builds upon nature, grace perfects nature, and grace elevates nature beyond itself.

St. Gertrude of Helfta, whom Pope Benedict XIV called "the Great," describes how grace worked in her soul to bring about a new and stable spiritual state, which was the beginning of habits existing to a heroic degree. She was a Benedictine nun of twenty-six years old and walking through the cloister at the close of the day. Up until that point, she says, she lived in a "fortress of vain-glory and curiosity which [her] pride had raised up within [her]." Christ appeared before her, saying, "I will save you, I will deliver you; fear not. You have licked the dust with my enemies, and you have sucked honey amidst thorns; but now return to me—I will receive you, and inebriate you with the torrent of celestial delights." Gertrude's soul melted within her and she desired to approach Christ, but an enormous hedge of thorns grew up between them. It was so high and so long and so dense that she could see no way over it, around it, or through it. The thorny hedge, she realized, represented her faults and bad habits, which, though they might seem small to an outsider, in fact separated her from perfection. Christ reached through the hedge and took Gertrude's hand. He drew her to himself. Her soul then flowered in prayer:

You enlightened and softened my mind, detaching me powerfully, by an interior unction, from an inordinate love of this world, and from all my vanities, so that . . . You alone were pleasing to my soul. And I praise, bless, adore, and thank from my inmost soul, as far as I am able, but not as far as I ought, your wise mercy and your merciful wisdom that you, my Creator and Redeemer, did endeavor in so loving a manner to submit my unconquerable self-opinionated habits to the sweetness of your yoke. I began to accomplish the work you set before me, which now became sweet and light, though a little while before appeared hard and almost unbearable.

Thus we may see how grace enables us to live up to our full potential by restoring what was lost by sin and by adding a new supernatural participation in God's life of superabundant excellence.

Whereas grace is a general supernatural habit that affects one's very being, faith is the habit that God infuses into the soul that perfects and elevates the mind to know the highest truths, especially the truth that the blessed will see and enjoy God eternally. By living faith, a believer assents firmly and absolutely to what God has said because God never deceives, for he is the luminous truth itself. Sometimes God speaks through his prophets, as seen in Moses, Jeremiah, and Isaiah. At other times, God speaks through the Magisterium of the Catholic Church when she declares a truth of faith or morals to be accepted by all believers. Faith gives the mind a certitude and firmness greater than any other truth, for it rests on God's unerring authority and trustworthiness. Because knowing God is nothing other than eternal life, faith begins eternal life in us even now. Faith reveals our final goal, which is heaven, as well as the chief means to reach it. In doing so, faith teaches the substances of everything necessary for living rightly. By uniting us with the mind of Christ, who was absolutely holy, faith provides us with the principles for overcoming temptation, and by doing so, it creates the possibility for purity of heart. For all these reasons, Aquinas says, faith precedes all other good habits in their fullness and opens the door to holiness.

Charity is the bright fire that warms and enlivens all habits, enabling them to become truly heroic. It is the virtue God infuses into the soul so that a person might love the Holy Trinity above all things, and love one's neighbor for God's sake. Merely emotional love is the passion by which we desire whatever seems pleasing to us, or by which we attract to ourselves whatever we think will benefit us. Charity transcends passions because it involves a choice of the will informed by faith. Through the grace and faith won by Christ, charity enables us to love God as a friend. This supernatural love of God can be understood as a participation in the Holy Spirit, who is "poured into our hearts," in the words of St. Paul (Rom 5:5). Christ directs charity in a fourfold way, saying, "You shall love the Lord your God with all your heart, and with all your soul, and with all your mind, and with all your strength" (Mk 12:30). Thomas explains that this command regards the perfection *necessary for salvation*, explaining it phrase by phrase. First, we should order our entire life to God with all our hearts. Second, we should love

God by believing whatever has been divinely transmitted to us. Third, we should shape all of our emotions through our love of God. Fourth, we should establish all our works in divine charity.

Love is not a hot mess. Being "in love" might feel like enduring a hurricane-level wind that threatens to destroy everything in its path, but human and divine love are naturally ordered. Aquinas explains that we always love some things more, some things less. Some people receive more of our heart's heat, others feel only a candle's worth of warmth. This reflects the order in our choice of love. The *subjective order* of love is the priority we voluntarily generate, as when a person prefers one friend to another. The *objective order* of love is the priority that exists among people and objects deserving of our love; it calls us to order our subjective preferences to it.

We have already seen the first and most important principle for ordering our love, understood as charity: we ought to love God above all things. As Christ said, "He who loves father or mother more than me is not worthy of me; and he who loves son or daughter more than me is not worthy of me; and he who does not take his cross and follow me is not worthy of me" (Mt 10:37–38). Christ also spoke about "hating" one's family, even one's own life (see Lk 14:26), but he did not mean willing them evil or rejecting them in some absolute sense. Rather, we must be ready to sacrifice any love for a creature if it gravely interferes with, or impedes, our love of God. To love God above all things is the "greatest and first commandment" (Mt 22:38). There is a second, which is "like" the first; namely, "you shall love your neighbor as yourself" (Mt 22:39; see Lv 19:18).

Good love and bad love are strict opposites: there is a love that energizes, elevates, and perfects, and there is a disfigured love—which really is not love at all—that depletes, drags down, and destroys. The right way to love one's neighbor is by taking into account who he really is. Projection of one's desires onto another person cannot lead to true love. The fundamental reality about our neighbor is his identity as person, a unique rational animal that reflects the very nature of God's wise and loving nature. Accordingly, the command to love our neighbor is "like" the command to love God because all humans are made in the image of God. Further-more, by loving our neighbor rightly, we can both manifest our love for God and increase our overall love: "If any one says, 'I love God,' and hates his brother, he is a liar; for he who does not love his brother whom he has seen, cannot love God whom he has not seen" (1 Jn 4:20). In the words of Aquinas, "It can be argued that, if any man does not love his neighbor, neither does he love God—not because his neigh-bor is more lovable, but because he is the first we encounter who calls for our love, for God is more lovable by reason of His greater goodness."

Developing Heroic Habits

Although heroic habits in the fullest sense require the direct action of God to infuse the soul with grace and virtue, no one can slouch into greatness. The heresy of Pelagianism supposes that we can initiate supernatural greatness by our own power. Equally problematic, though less discussed, is the contrary heresy of Quietism, which proposes that we should sit back and let God "take the wheel" of life so that we contribute little or nothing to our perfection. Augustine expressed the balanced and correct view with his well-known observation: "God who created you without your help, will not save you without your effort." The same is true for habits. God who creates the conditions for heroic habits will not give them growth without our heroic efforts. The infused virtues are habits because they are latent inclinations to perform acts directed to the triune God. But these habits are like seeds planted in our soul; they will not grow, flourish, or bear fruit on their own. We need to cultivate them with our activity to ensure that grace waters them well.

To understand our contribution toward developing heroic habits, we can consider their natural conditions as explained by the science of expertise and training for optimal performance. For most of human history, athletes and soldiers could achieve performance only by relying on such factors as luck, anecdotal advice sifted by time, and the directions of coaches. Undoubtedly, these helped people achieve great things. More recently, however, there has been a systematic study of the broad conditions that lead to greatness. Michael Sherwin identifies five traits common to all expert-level habits.

1. A standard of excellence according to which an action is judged as successful or unsuccessful.
2. The internalization or "realization" of the standards that guide the structure of the activity—for example, the rules of chess, the grammar of a language, the Ten Commandments, etc.
3. Fidelity to an expert model, for beginners need to

be guided by masters, who show the proper way to practice.

4. The social context of learning, in which one's knowledge is tested by a master and displayed to a public.

5. Expertise itself understood as a creative freedom for excellence manifested in right activity.

Sherwin's assessment is bolstered by an increasing body of evidence that provides precision and objective measures to our understanding of expertise. Skills related to sports, for instance, perfect a person's native powers of movement: long-distance racing perfects a person's ability to run; basketball perfects the ability to jump; weight training perfects the ability to lift and carry.

Researchers have found that natural physical advantage *aids* elite performance: heart size for long-distance cyclists, hand size for basketball players, leg to waist ratio for runners, and so on. What makes the *greatest* difference, however, is how athletes understand and use their bodies when compared to athletes with comparable physical traits. They do this by "preserved cognitive control of expert performance." Theirs is more than brute force. It is the habituated "ability to consistently reproduce the same motor actions" by the conscious control of fine movements, with the ability to vary performance in a flexible manner as needed. Research indicates that "expert performance is mediated by acquired mental representations that allow the experts to anticipate, plan, and reason alternative courses of action." Experts gain advantages over competitors by cultivating a careful analysis of their own state in action—physiological, emotional, mental—and in doing so, they gain a more precise knowledge and understanding of expert performance. This enables them to articulate a better description of the performance context, such as a basketball game, which in turn helps them better predict the consequences of their actions and their opponents' actions. These mental representations help the expert assert more direct influence over his lower powers, including "the complex mechanisms that control perception, attention, and memory, which allow expert athletes to gain their performance advantage in dynamically changing game situations."

Significantly, studies show that expert performance even of physical tasks such as playing soccer or shooting a gun is primarily a training of the mind in light of an exemplary model. Expertise is developed when a person establishes practice tasks wherein planning and consequent action can be evaluated against the actions of expert performers in similar situations. The high school basketballer critiques his game performance by comparison with Michael Jordan and LeBron James. Royal Navy captains consider their seamanship in light of Lord Nelson's seamanship. In some ways, an expert could be called a hero in the realm of his expertise: "Louis Armstrong is my hero," a jazz enthusiast might say; a chess player might reply, "Gary Kasparov is my hero." Greater heroism goes further: it exists on a supernatural level with fully Christlike virtues that make a person as a whole possess heroic habits. Those who strive for heroic habits consider what the greatest heroes would do. This is where the examples of the saints shine like stars in the night sky to guide us on our way.

St. Jerome's struggles helpfully illustrate how vigorous expert training operates with grace. He is considered to be one of the greatest Church Fathers, a "Doctor" or universal teacher to Christians, a "model of conduct and teacher of the human race," in the words of Pope Benedict XVI. On the side of training for optimal performance, it has been noted that "Jerome took considerable pride in the fact that he was not self-taught" but rather learned from Donatus, a pinnacle of grammarians in his time. From childhood, Jerome took pains to master the Roman classic authors, including Virgil, Terence, and Cicero. In time, he became a virtuoso in Latin expression. Yet with a charming frankness, Jerome described how difficult it was to develop good habits of character and learning in Sacred Scripture. In a letter to a friend, he wrote:

> When I was a young man, though I was protected by the rampart of the lonely desert, I could not endure the promptings of sin and the ardent heat of my nature. I tried to crush them by frequent fasting, but my mind was always a turmoil of imagination. To subdue it I put myself in the hands of one of the brethren who had been a Hebrew before his conversion, and asked him to teach me his language. . . . What efforts I spent on that task, what difficulties I had to face, how often I despaired, how often I gave up and then in my eagerness to learn began again, my own knowledge can witness from personal experience and those can testify who were then living with me. I thank the Lord that from a bitter seed of learning I am now plucking sweet fruits.

In a different letter, Jerome recounted a terrifying revelation in which he learned the true state of his soul. It was the middle of Lent, when in a vision, he came before the heavenly judgment seat. Asked who and what he was, Jerome replied, "I am a Christian." But he who presided said, "You lie. You are a follower of Cicero, not of Christ. For 'where your treasure is, there will your heart be also.'" After the alarming vision, Jerome awoke and testified, "Henceforth I read the books of God with a greater zeal than I had ever given before to the books of men." Jerome's experience bears many lessons for us, not least that heroic habits are like the cedars of Lebanon: unlike Jack's beanstalk, they do not grow overnight. They require time, energy, and nourishment for their development. For a theological virtue to grow, one must make acts appropriate to that virtue: to increase one's faith, one must make acts of faith; to grow in charity, one must actually love God and neighbor.

In a previous chapter, we saw how St. John Henry Newman's faith in the claims of the Catholic Church came about through his fidelity to the truth and his study of the Church Fathers such as St. Basil the Great, St. Gregory Nazianzen, St. Athanasius, and others. The more acts of faith one makes, or the more intensely one makes such acts, the more one increases in faith. One makes an act of faith only when one chooses to do so: God does not force us to believe in him, and the Church has no power to induce us to accept her preaching. All Catholics possess faith to some degree, but the heroic habit of faith may be discerned from particular acts that manifest faith, or in persistent faith amid great difficulties. In the canonization process of Peter of Alcantara, witnesses testified that he would not have hesitated to die for a single point of the Creed: "In his mind no certainty, evidence, or clear conviction, could even distantly approach to the certainty which he had of the infallible truth of our holy faith, against which he never had any temptation . . . that not even revelations could make him swaver, or swerve in the slightest degree from what the Catholic Church holds and sets forth, and the sacred Scriptures teach."

Heroic faith shines out in great firmness and steadfastness, as well as in the fervent desire that the truth be spread so that all peoples may know and love the holy truths taught by faith. Thus, a high degree of faith is seen in those who taught the faith however they could, by establishing schools or by preaching in mission territory, or by fighting heresies through writing.

The growth of infused habits follows the familiar path of the habit loop: (a) fidelity to truth constitutes an antecedent that prepares the soul to (b) perform the behavior of an ordinary act of faith, such as professing the Nicene Creed with true assent, which then prepares the soul to (c) make an act of extraordinary faith, such as teaching Catholic truths even in trying circumstances.

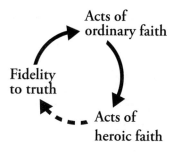

Charity can also grow: indeed, in this life, charity has the potential for continual growth. The saints recognized the importance of making frequent and conscious prayers of love to God, bolstered by little sacrifices. Charity-bolstering acts include frequently and piously speaking about God; continually meditating on the Catholic faith, especially the mysteries of Christ's passion; fervent and purposeful acts of love toward God such as "Oh God, I love you with all my heart" or as St. Alphonsus Liguori would say, "Let me love you more and more!"; heavy distress on account of the absence of Christ; and joyful fulfillment of the difficult demands of religion out of love for God. Lambertini notes that heroic charity may be inferred if a person frequently performs such acts frequently, promptly, easily, and with pleasure, in difficult circumstances especially at the risk of life, honor, or significant property.

St. Thérèse of Lisieux illustrates how charity can grow in the soul. When she was a child, her mother, St. Zélie, wrote, "Even Thérèse is anxious to make sacrifices. Marie has given her little sisters a string of beads on purpose to count their acts of self-denial. . . . [She] put[s] her hand in her pocket, time after time, to pull a bead along the string, whenever she makes a little sacrifice." As she grew up, the habit of self-sacrifice out of love of God became so natural in the soul that she no longer needed to count them. All of this prepared her for the moment when she would make her "Self-Offering to Merciful Love," which reads in part: "O My God! Most Blessed Trinity, I desire to Love you and make you Loved, to work for the glory of Holy Church by saving souls on earth and liberating those suffering in purgatory. I desire to accomplish your will perfectly and to reach the degree of glory you have prepared for me in your kingdom. I desire, in a word, to be a Saint, but I feel my helplessness and I beg you, O my God! to be yourself my Sanctity!"

Once again, we see that the God-focused fire of charity is crucial for heroic habits. By uniting us to God as our highest good and best love, charity focuses everything in our life on God, including our habits, dispositions, and skills. In the words of St. Paul, it is the "bond of perfection" (Col 3:15). Charity sets our habits aflame with divine love, acting as a furnace in which they are gradually perfected. As charity becomes more perfect, it also comes to take command of all our acts and habits. The gradual perfection of all habits therefore corresponds to the stages of the perfection of charity. Following ancient tradition, Aquinas describes the growth of charity as belonging to three states: beginners, the proficient, and "the perfect." These have been magnificently explained by Reginald Garrigou-Lagrange in *Three Ages of the Spiritual Life* and in the classic work by St. Bonaventure called *The Triple Way*. Here, then, I will merely summarize the stages, which can be compared to the way fire gradually burns wood.

First, fire acts upon green wood by heating it up and expelling all interior moisture. Through this "purgative" process, wood is "purified" of interior moisture. In this process, the wood becomes black with charcoal, similar to how a person sometimes seems *worse* in the first stages of the spiritual life as he realizes his imperfections. During this stage, it is important for a person to carefully consider his habits in the light of faith, to pray that they be purified by charity, and to let go of any habits by asceticism if they are contrary to holiness. The hissing and popping sounds of burning wood mark the escape of steam, much like a person sighing at the pain of being detached from a disordered love for worldly things.

Second, fire sets the wood alight. Just as wood begins to give off a faint light of its own, so in this "illuminative" stage, the soul both receives greater light from God and it begins faintly to shine forth to others. Once some of the obstacles of charity have been cleared away by purification, a person will want to focus more on growth in the virtues, actively cultivating them in a way that helps him accomplish the duties of his state of life. Because the fire is barely glowing in this stage, a person will be careful to tend the flame and ensure that it receives just enough fuel to remain alight but not so much as to overwhelm it and snuff it out. Hence, one will avoid lukewarmness by feeding his soul with the sacraments and the prayer of contemplation, as well as with works of charity. He will also avoid burdening himself with excessive spiritual activities, for which his love and energy may not be adequate.

Third, fire transforms wood entirely into flame so that only a blaze remains in this "unitive" stage. Those who have been transformed by charity desire "to be dissolved and to be with Christ." In this stage, purifications and illuminations continue but in a higher register as the soul ascends closer and closer to the state which it will enjoy for eternity. Here, human nature remains, though in an elevated state, such that the person radiates the heat and light of God's love and seems to be another Christ. In this stage, as the developing saint experiences greater transforming union with God, the Gifts of the Holy Spirit become more predominant in his life. A person in this stage spends longer hours in prayer, achieves greater apostolic works, and becomes transformed into a sort of divine fire.

Here, too, the habit loop is a useful model. (a) Purification of the soul helps to prepare it for (b) illumination and the proper acts that spread God's light to others, which in turn disposes the soul for (c) union with God and the deepening effects and acts of heroic virtue.

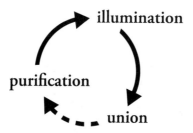

The dotted line indicates that union with God in this life does not remove the need for further purification. On the contrary, those who love God deeply seek to be ever more purified of whatever separates themselves from him. This cycle continues until death.

It is important to insist that the love of God spills over into the love of neighbor, of which there are three basic aspects. First, we should love our neighbor for God's sake. Aquinas beautifully explains what it means to love one thing or person "for the sake" of another: "When a man has friendship for a certain person, for his sake he loves all belonging to him, be they children, servants, or connected with him in any way. Indeed, so much do we love our friends, that for their sake we love all who belong to them, even if they hurt or hate us; so that, in this way, the friendship of charity extends even to our enemies, whom we love out of charity in relation to God, to Whom the friendship of charity is chiefly directed."

We can see this sort of "directed love" in marriage: a husband's love for his wife can be so expansive that it extends to the rest of her family, impelling him even to care for his mother-in-law in her old age. Likewise, a wife's love for her husband comes to include genuine care for his parents and even his annoying little brother.

Second, to love someone well, we should try to please him or her in what is legitimate, though we should not capitulate to our neighbor's every desire: "a man should not give way to his neighbor in evil, but only in good things, even as he ought to gratify his will in good things alone."

Third, true love for another excludes motives of selfish gain and mere pleasure. Rather, we should love our neighbor for his own good, which ultimately means hoping and working for his salvation. This true love acts not in some obtuse, badgering way but according to what will truly help the love of God flower in his heart and bear fruit in eternal life.

It is not always easy to identify exterior acts that manifest heroic charity for one's neighbor. Ladling soup for the poor can be an expression of mere philanthropy—a mere *love of human beings* with no transcendent motive—or it can be an expression of divine charity. This is because it is the interior reality of the agent's motives which vivifies the acts, focusing them on either worldly or heavenly ends. Mercy is the chief act of charity. The works of mercy manifest charity when they are performed out of love of God and love for the soul of one's neighbor. Hence, exterior corporal works of mercy, such as feeding the poor, caring for the sick, visiting those in prison, and so on are less manifestly enlivened by love for Christ than the spiritual works of mercy, such as counseling the doubtful, teaching the ignorant, correcting those in error, and so on—acts that more directly stem from faith. Thus, St. Teresa of Calcutta insisted that the merciful charity of her religious order was to be well-ordered by the light of faith. The Missionaries of Charity truly exercise charity, she said. They are more than social workers; they bring the love of Christ to the world and see the face of Christ in those they serve.

Heroic Habits in Different Shapes and Sizes

Not all who possess heroic habits do things that most people would think are great. There are not a few "simple" saints who apparently had mediocre or even deficient natural talents. One might think of St. Benedict Joseph Labre, the patron of vagrants, or any number of "holy fools," such as St. Simeon of Emesa, and pious children, such as Little Nellie of Cork and Bl. Imelda Lambertini. But a lack of astounding deeds need not signify a soul bereft of excellence.

Even in the world of natural heroism, some forms of greatness are incompatible with others. Greatness of soul, for instance, often shuns exteriorly great deeds in order to focus on stoking an interior fire. This may be seen in the famous incident in which Alexander the Great visited the philosopher Diogenes of Sinope, whom he admired. While

Diogenes was lying in the sun, Alexander approached and asked if there was anything he could give him. Already the warrior had conquered much of Greece, Egypt, Babylon, and significant parts of what is now Turkey and India. He had at hand wealth, warriors, and untold power. Diogenes raised himself a little and replied, "Yes, there is something you can do for me. Stand aside and stop blocking the sun." Alexander was struck by this answer. He was so surprised by the philosopher's greatness, since he cared little for worldly things, he said that if he were not Alexander, he would choose to be Diogenes. The man replied, "If I were not Diogenes, I would choose to be Diogenes too."

Not all forms of greatness are compatible with others. A warrior typically does not have sufficient time, peace, and resources to become a deep scholar; a sports star is almost never an epoch-making mathematician. Each has his own way to greatness. Each must strive to make his own plot of land fruitful, however big or small it might be. Sometimes God will grant graces that supplement a person's deficiencies, as when St. Peter's preaching at Pentecost could be understood in many languages though he spoke only one, or as when St. John Vianney and St. Padre Pio were given supernatural insight into the souls of penitents in the confessional, or when St. Joseph of Cupertino's notorious mental stuntedness was offset by incredible miracles of healing and flight. But the greatness of these saints was not in their miracles. It was in their souls, which achieved a heroism appropriate for their condition, time, and place. Garrigou-Lagrange puts it well: "All must climb toward the summit of perfection by opposite slopes; the meek must learn to become strong, and the strong to become meek. Thus the acquired and the infused virtues should complete man's excellent natural inclinations and combat the numerous defects which sully his moral character. . . . It is essential to know how to play the keyboard of the virtues without sounding false notes, without confounding meekness with cowardice, and magnanimity with pride."

It bears repeating that the most heroic heroism is heroism of the soul. In the battleground of the soul, a person can find true heroism by conquering the warring hordes of evil within himself, overcoming sin, vice, and even the demons who try to overpower his strength and make him their eternal slave. Each person is a *microcosm*, a little universe, and a person who conquers himself conquers a world: "He who is slow to anger is better than the mighty, and he who rules his spirit than he who takes a city" (Prv 16:32).

Now we may reconsider the example of St. Thomas Aquinas. He shows us that even bookish friars with matching personalities can achieve a heroism that befits their natures. Although Thomas never served as a missionary to faraway lands, nor worked in hospitals, nor performed any of the flashy actions that gain praise from crowds, he was nevertheless imbued with extraordinary holiness. He manifested his holiness in a great love of the Eucharist, such that before writing on the Blessed Sacrament, he would visit Christ in the chapel and lean his head against the tabernacle. When struggling to understand a particularly difficult passage from the prophet Isaiah, he did not rely on his gigantic intellect but fasted and prayed until God answered him. At least once, God even sent Sts. Peter and Paul to teach him. Despite

Thomas's vast literary output, whose depth has not been exhausted after eight centuries, he remained meek and humble, never looking for honors or powerful positions. Anyone who knows university professors knows that humility is an almost infallible sign of heroic virtue for intellectuals.

CHAPTER 6

DEVILISH HABITS

God has never wanted to limit the glory of man. The grace that God offers us is not measured according to our merits but according to his infinite riches as benefactor. God, notwithstanding the indignity of us creatures, shows that he loves us more than the rest of his works—to the point where one could doubt his wisdom more easily than his goodness.

Although fashioned from clay, we were destined to be like unto God in all things. Made in his image, we were to be transformed from glory to glory, until his very goodness shone through us. Through union with the Holy Trinity by grace, we were to share in God's own life, being, excellence, power, goodness, beauty, and all of his other infinite perfections. Unrefined iron is cold, dark, hard, and without beauty on its own. When thrust into a furnace and penetrated by the heat of a great fire, the iron appears bright, warm, and supple without losing its own nature. That was our destiny, but by sin we cast ourselves away from the divine presence. Without the beauty of holiness, our souls grow cold, dark, and hard. Bad habits fix us in that state, like a man trapped in an iron box encased in ice and dropped into the bitter sea.

In this way, the greatness of our vocation reveals the gravity of sin and vice.

St. Catherine of Siena caught wind of the disgusting nature of evil in another way. Once, she visited the court of Pope Gregory IX. While speaking with him, she remarked that the Roman Curia should be a paradise of virtue, but instead she smelled the stench of the vices of hell. This was no metaphor. A previous time, she and her confessor, Bl. Raymond of Capua, talked with a lovely woman who had an honest face and acted modestly. Later on, St. Catherine said to the Dominican friar: "If you were able to smell the stench that I smelled coming off her while we were talking, you would have vomited." The woman, despite appearances, was a priest's concubine.

In this chapter, I am going to discuss the nature of devilish habits: how they develop, what role is played by evil thoughts, and how we can overcome them with the help of Christ. We will find that the highway to hell looks suspiciously like a habit loop pointed away from God and toward some distorted end.

Becoming Wicked: the Six Stages of a Bad Habit

Different kinds of cancer have different rates of growth: skin cancer generally is slower, whereas lung and liver cancer are faster. Few kill overnight. Similarly, vice is a habit, and like all habits, it does not develop in a single moment. Like cancer in the soul, vice grows over time. In an instant, a single mortal sin, like theft, can kill the soul by separating a person from God, the principle of life-giving grace. But a single sin may be an isolated act, uncharacteristic of the person. Becoming a thief—that is, becoming an expert in the dangerous art of theft—requires time and commitment. I know this from a firsthand account. Once, a prisoner in a super-maximum-security prison lamented that his sister had just been put into the clink. I asked what happened, and he said, "She was trying to rob a store, and the alarm went off. Her friends drove away, and she was left stranded. Before she could get out of there, the cops showed up. She's so dumb," he continued. "She doesn't know anything about alarms and security cameras. She's an amateur. Not like me! I could tell you all about it, but I guess that doesn't grab you, does it, Father?" It didn't grab me. But that conversation often reminds me of how virtue and vice are never stable characteristics. They are either growing or shrinking within us.

Vice develops along a fairly predictable path. As the prophet Hosea said about Israel, "They sow the wind, and they shall reap the whirlwind" (Hos 8:7). Thomas Aquinas helps us to see that if we sow sin, we will reap the habit of vice. Synthesizing the thought of St. Jerome and St. Gregory the Great, Aquinas wrote that wickedness develops in a six-stage process: from thoughts to words, from words to deeds, from deeds to the state of incontinence, from incontinence to full-blown vice, and

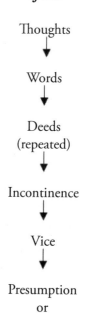

Hell-bound Path of Sin

Thoughts
↓
Words
↓
Deeds
(repeated)
↓
Incontinence
↓
Vice
↓
Presumption
or
Despair

from vice to despair or presumption. These are organically connected, like the roots, trunk, branches, flowers, and fruits of a poisonous tree. Here, I will examine each stage, focusing on thoughts as the beginning and root of chosen evil, bad moral habits, and vice.

(1) Evil Thoughts

The downward spiral of vice begins when a person voluntarily harbors disordered thoughts and corresponding desires. A lack of order characterizes the undisciplined mind, with serious moral consequences.

Mental disorder can exist in three basic ways: connections, processes, and content. These are related to what Thomas Dubay calls "give-away traits of the nonthinker."

Disorder of the least problematic sort involves *disconnections* among thoughts, whereby the undisciplined mind, like an attic full of dusty items haphazardly stuffed in it, harbors sentiments, fantasies, memories, partial insights, crude judgments, opinions, real expertise, and prejudices heaped together in an unintelligible mess. In this case, Dubay notes, a person can be sluggishly comfortable with contradictory opinions, with no wisp of a desire to reconcile them. Here, we might think of activists simultaneously proclaiming, in Orwellian fashion, "we support inclusion for all" and "we must exclude badthink." Some of this disorder can be overcome through education in logic, metaphysics, and theology.

More pernicious mental disorder arises in *processes* of thought. A widespread process-disorder of the mind is simply *not thinking*. Many people allow feelings and images to move them and do not bother to think about life deeply, or to offer thought-out reasons for their opinions. This sort of person denies reason its rightful kingly rule over the emotions and imagination and instead allows the senses to run riot. Such a mind will be rather unaffected by evidence against one's opinions. Having observed many such persons in the wild, I propose a bestiary of mindless monsters that presently prowl about the world.

- *Zombies*: These people are seemingly mentally alive but in fact are only in a state of vivified death. They can attack another's ideas but are infected with a thought virus and have no real life of the mind, and thus almost no individuality. A rioting mob exemplifies a zombie-like state of existence; their behavior has been compared to a "non-playable character" in a video game. Difficult to stop in their onward cannibalistic lurching, zombies are perhaps the most destructive group of nonthinkers in the short term.

- *Robots*: The difference between a zombie and a robot is that a robot lives by rules, whereas a zombie is essentially lawless, anarchical. Unthinking, unfeeling bureaucrats can be compared to robots. They will often fulfill their duty punctiliously—albeit with glitches of arbitrariness that always happen to benefit themselves or their friends, often resulting in less work. While seeming more harmless than zombies, they are very powerful when they become killer robots.

- *Vampires*: More sophisticated and sentient than zombies or robots, vampires of the mind nevertheless are not fully alive; they are only "undead." When younger, they were alive, but if they did not fight off the vampires they attracted by their beauty or talent, they entered into the system of victim and victimizer. A vampire feeds on the lifeblood of others to avoid death. Vampires thus live by a pyramid scheme of blackmail, as in the mayor who takes credit for an idea upon which a congresswoman feasted, without acknowledging the speechwriter who got the idea from a professor who got the idea from Marx; a content "creator" who sells the work of a programmer, who was remixing material he "borrowed" from a college roommate; a businessman who vacuums up the talent of intelligent subordinates while threatening to fire them if their creativity disagrees with his ideology. All of these operate by alternating threats and rewards to keep their victims in check while they bleed them dry. This sort of person is the most seductive nonthinker.

- *Werewolves*: Werewolves are two-faced agents. By day, they act rationally, often because their job and ordinary life depends on it. By night, however, they display a wolfish side that overpowers their reason and attacks the rational order of the world. For example, a khaki-sporting school teacher who sips a Starbucks soy mocha latte by day might don a black hoodie by night and attack the very same left-leaning coffee vendor because of "inequality."

Thus, the werewolf is violent when the animal is released, reflecting the violence of an unreconciled dual existence. This sort of person is confusing and dangerous to himself and to others.

- *Clowns*: This group is relatively small, but they garner more than warranted attention because they are the loudest, and the most manifestly ridiculous. A cartoon or clown is often recognizable by her garish hair and clothing: she is a veritable walking canvas of absurdist art, a conformist version of rebellion. Sometimes a clown is recognizable just by the red nose he puts on while wearing otherwise respectable clothing. Clowns seem to be harmless fools who provide a side-show of entertainment. But everyone should fear a killer clown because they will carry a dagger behind their smile.

- *Sleepwalkers*: Unlike zombies, sleepwalkers don't evidence having any ideas at all, nor much movement. They perform only the minimal actions necessary for life and then return to their sleep-state, connected to the matrix of distraction devices—phones, video games, computers, televisions, marijuana, alcohol, and so on. These sorts of persons probably constitute the largest portion of society.

The common trait of these mental monsters is that *they don't think*. John Paul II was surely correct when he said, "Driven by the desire to discover the ultimate truth of existence, human beings seek to acquire those universal elements of knowledge which enable them to understand themselves better and to advance in their own self-realization. These fundamental elements of knowledge spring from the *wonder* awakened in them by the contemplation of creation." This is true for humans in general. We have an innate drive for the truth, and for happiness. But in particular individuals, especially in our contemporary soporific world, good drives can become mutilated or muted. Instead of being awake with wonder, a sadly large number are hypnotized and buffered from the vigor and beauty of nature.

Finally, a person can harbor thoughts that are themselves disordered because they depart from the order of reality. Such thoughts include culpable mistakes, half-truths, errors, and falsehoods. Dubay wisely points out that such persons often have a penchant for jargon, slogans, labels, and name-calling—all of which are examples of mental laziness and arrogance substituting for understanding, nuanced thought, or silence when humility would call for it. This leads us to consider the problematic content of bad thoughts.

The ancient monk Evagrius noted that there are eight kinds of demons that tempt us with eight kinds of wicked thoughts, which lead to eight kinds of evil deeds. In his *Disputed Questions on Evil*, Thomas drew upon later tradition and discussed Seven Deadly Sins, with the eighth, pride, as the "mother" that gives birth to them all. A number of modern authors have discussed them well, so I will not address them here. Instead, it may be useful to note a few other thoughts, the behavior they lead to, the consequences they entail, and what Christian thoughts should occupy our minds instead.

Antecedent thought	Behavior	Consequent	Remedies: Christian thoughts
My action is not *very bad.*	Sin in speech or deed	Corruption of the soul	God is the true judge of a sin's gravity; even small sins can lead to hell.
God is *merciful*; he won't mind if I sin			God is as just as he is merciful; God's mercy should induce us to ask forgiveness for past sins, not to commit future sins.
I can always *repent.*			Repentance is very difficult; many have died before repenting.
Others *get away with* worse actions.			Everyone will receive their just reward in the end; we should compare ourselves to saints, not sinners.

Chapter four explained how erroneous judgments of events can lead to various emotions that lead to corresponding exterior actions as consequents. To eradicate evil thoughts, the roots of all sin and vice, we must also identify their causes, as indicated in the Gospel: "Jesus, knowing their thoughts, said, 'Why do you think evil in your hearts?'" (Mt 9:4). Demons are among the causes, for they whisper wicked thoughts in our ears. But an individual should shoulder his portion of culpability as well. Personal causes for a polluted mind include:

- a lack of serious thinking and study,
- a love for fads, a desire to remain mainstream and socially acceptable,
- the darkening effects of sin, which clouds the mind,
- seeking preferences rather than evidence,

- submission to political-commercial propaganda,
- ignorance of truths necessary for developing good habits,
- contempt of truths of the faith,
- distraction, especially a lack of attention to spiritual things.

Christ explains the foundational cause: "*Out of the heart come evil thoughts*" (Mt 15:19; emphasis added). That is, disordered desires of the heart lead to evil thoughts; evil thoughts likewise produce and strengthen evil desires. Thought and desire are like body and soul, closer than twins, affecting each other in inextricable ways.

Ancient wisdom advises us to "fight fire with fire," or "like with like." Evagrius wisely notes that to overcome disordered passions, and memories that stir up our passions, we must tame our bodily desiring and assertive appetites (concupiscible and irascible) by means of *bodily asceticism*, such as fasting, vigils, and sleeping on the ground. However, to overcome bad thoughts, one must cultivate good thoughts: "Evil thoughts cut off good ones, and in turn evil ones are cut off by good ones." Christian thoughts, derived from faith and enlivened by charity, are remedies for disordered interior thoughts that dwell in our intellects. If they are not cultivated, then evil words will eventually spill from our lips.

(2) Evil Words

The second stage in the corruptive progression of evil is when thoughts and desires manifest themselves in speech.

To grasp the essential features of speech, and to measure the gravity of wicked words, we can turn to the prologue to the Gospel of John: "In the beginning was the Word, and the Word was with God, and the Word was God. . . . And the Word became flesh and dwelt among us, full of grace and truth" (Jn 1:1, 14).

Commenting on this passage, Aquinas follows Augustine and explains that for every rational being, there can be an *interior* word and an *exterior* word. The interior word is that which the mind conceives; the exterior word is that which the mouth expresses. The second Person of the Holy Trinity is called the Word of God because the Father eternally conceives of the Word in his thought. We conceive of ideas, thoughts, in time, with imperfection, as existing within our mind. God conceives of the single Word within timeless eternity, in absolute perfection, as a substantial Word that exists with divine nature: he is equal to God. As St. John of the Cross beautifully expressed, "In giving us his Son, his only Word (for he possesses no other), [God the Father] spoke everything to us at once in this sole Word—and he has no more to say." God's Word became *exteriorized* and expressed in time when the Word became flesh and dwelt among us. God's incarnate Word, who is Jesus Christ, is "full of grace and truth," and so all our finite spoken words should be without evil or error and instead entirely gracious and truthful. God's Word "was life, and the life was the light of men" (Jn 1:4). Likewise, all our expressed words should stem from an abiding union with God, and with God's help, they can be "enfleshed" in the world, strengthening the life of others and enlightening their minds with the beauty and goodness of truth.

Thomas notes that "a word from the mouth shows forth and announces whatever is in the soul, because spoken words are a sign of movements of the soul. A good word indicates a good interior disposition, but an evil word indicates an evil disposition." As Christ said, "For out of the abundance of the heart the mouth speaks" (Mt 12:34). Like a boil tight with pus, evil interior thoughts and desires press to burst forth in exterior words. Aquinas explains that those who speak evilly do so from an abundance because undoubtedly they hold back at least some of their evil thoughts. What they did not fear to let loose was only a lesser portion of the infection kept inside. The spiritual result is fearsome: "I tell you," Jesus attests, "on the day of judgment men will render account for every careless word they utter; for by your words you will be justified, and by your words you will be condemned" (Mt 12:36–37). Not only will pernicious, vile speech be condemned but also every single frivolous word said without purpose will testify against one's character and reveal the hidden caverns of the heart on judgment day. Accordingly, Sacred Scripture teaches, "Death and life are in the power of the tongue" (Prv 18:21), and, "An evil man is ensnared by the transgression of his lips" (Prv 12:13).

Following Aquinas, we can describe sins of speech as against God, oneself, and one's neighbor. Into these broad categories fit the various "wicked tongues," identified by St. Thomas of Villanova.

Against God:

- The *blasphemous* tongue, which mocks and speaks wickedly of God and holy things.
- The *ungrateful* tongue, which doesn't praise and thank others, especially God, but instead derides the good one has received.

Against oneself:

- The *never-ending* tongue, which yaps unceasingly.
- The *bombastic* tongue, which is employed by the arrogant for flowery speech, or by the histrionic to blurt out uncontrolled emotions.

Against one's neighbor:

- The *crafty* tongue, which aids the duplicitous and treacherous.
- The *poisonous* tongue, possessed by the envious and detractors.
- The *forked* tongue in liars, perjurers, pretenders, and those who give false testimony.
- The *alluring* tongue, meant to gain favor by charming but empty words.
- The *lewd* tongue, used by seducers and the bawdy.
- The *iniquitous* tongue, skillfully twisted by flatterers.
- The *sharp* tongue of the angry and bitter who attack others unjustly.
- The *misleading* tongue, seen especially in unscrupulous merchants, lawyers, and politicians.
- The *cursing* tongue, which intends to harm by calling down evil.

The notion of an evil sort of "tongue" indicates a certain habitual way of speaking. More than an accidental slip of the lip, one who has a "forked tongue" or a "bombastic tongue" has practiced this sort of speech frequently.

The ancient Jewish writer Philo compared a river to one's thoughts, and the banks of a river to one's lips, which are a sort of fence for one's tongue. When a person despises virtue but loves to look knowledgeable, his thoughts will often overflow their banks and escape as words which spread error and folly to the fields of other minds. In contrast, the lips of the righteous are gates that are thoughtfully opened to release measured words and establish "the irresistible strength of the better and true wisdom." Here, we might think of the many great saints who, like St. Paul, felt the urgency of charity compelling them to spread the truth about Christ.

St. Raymond Nonnatus, having entered the Mercedarian Order, went on a mission to Algeria to convert Muslims and ransom enslaved Christians. Choosing to be imprisoned to let a captive go free, Raymond preached to the captives and jailors alike, and even baptized two followers of Islam. To keep him from spreading the Gospel further, the captors bored a hole through his lips with a red-hot poker, then closed them with a padlock. For the next eight months, until he was eventually ransomed by his brothers, Raymond was allowed to open his mouth only every third day to eat. If only we were willing to "padlock" our lips when we were tempted to say something evil! Let us make the prayer of the psalmist our own: "Set a guard over my mouth, O LORD, keep watch over the door of my lips! Incline not my heart to any evil, to busy myself with wicked deeds" (Ps 141:3–4).

With mouths closed to evil words, we must open them to good words that edify and build up others (see Eph 4:29).

(3) Evil Deeds

Now we come to the third stage of evil—namely, exterior action—whereby a person deliberately acts in a disordered, sinful way. Sirach affirms that the interior word, thoughts, are the source of human action: "A word is the source of every deed; a thought, of every act" (Sir 37:16, NABRE). Evil thoughts often give rise to evil speech, but not always. Sometimes thoughts bypass speech and go directly to deeds. In either case, they tend to lead to the act of sin.

Comedians used to joke about a widespread Catholic sense of guilt, but nowadays it seems that many Catholics are as shameless as unbelievers. In 1948, Pope Pius XII said, "The sin of the century is the loss of the sense of sin." This is even truer today, for many reasons. A secularized world pervaded by images of evil has desensitized the mind to the disorder of sin, thereby blunting the prick of conscience. Within the Church, John Paul II pointed out, "Some are inclined to replace exaggerated attitudes of the past with other exaggerations. From seeing sin everywhere they pass to not recognizing it anywhere; from too much emphasis on the fear of eternal punishment they pass to preaching a love of God that excludes any punishment deserved by sin; from severity in trying to correct erroneous consciences they pass to a kind of respect for conscience which excludes the duty of telling the truth." The result is that many people commit sin unabashedly, with disastrous spiritual and temporal effects. To face this grave crisis, we must restore a proper sense of sin.

The classic phrase upon entering a confessional was "Forgive me, Father, for I have sinned." Sin is more than a thoughtless mistake. We might truthfully say, "I got into an accident." We do not say, "I *committed* an accident." An accident in this strict sense of the term is an unforeseen negative event that we suffer. In contrast, sin does not merely happen to us. Sin is a deliberate act we perform. It deviates from a proper order to the right end, working against the natural law, the rule of reason, or divine law. Focusing on the role of the will and its love, Augustine describes sin as an act of turning from the unchangeable good, which is God, and a turning toward a changeable good. Sin is something that ultimately stems from our personal, conscious, and free choice. Augustine explains, "Sin is the will to retain or pursue what justice forbids, and from which there is freedom to abstain; although if there is no freedom, there is no will," and consequently, no sin. Scripture attests that we must take responsibility for our chosen wrong:

> Do not say, "Because of the Lord I left the right way";
>   for he will not do what he hates.
> Do not say, "It was he who led me astray";
>   for he had no need of a sinful man. . . .
> It was he who created man in the beginning,
>   and he left him in the power of his own inclination.
> If you will, you can keep the commandments. . . .
> He has placed before you fire and water:
>   stretch out your hand for whichever you wish.

Before a man are life and death,
  and whichever he chooses will be given to him. (Sir
  15:11–12, 14–15, 16–17)

True followers of God therefore have always recognized
that their own choice plays the crucial factor for the existence of sin in their lives. In the words of the prodigal son,
"Father, I have sinned against heaven and before you" (Lk
15:18).

In chapter 2, we saw that human actions are primarily
measured by their object; secondarily, by their end; and,
lastly, by their circumstances. The object of the act defines the
act to be *this sort of action*, and not *that other* sort. Following
Aquinas, Pope John Paul II explained that "the morality of
the human act depends primarily and fundamentally on the
'object' rationally chosen by the deliberate will." The object
constitutes the objective aspect of the act, which John Paul
II identifies as "a freely chosen behavior" that serves as "the
proximate end of a deliberate decision which determines the
act of willing on the part of the acting person."

The object of murder, for instance, is the deliberate killing of an innocent person. Murder is always wrong. It can
never become good because the killer intends some good
outcome from it, such as receiving money from the killing to pay for his grandmother's heart surgery. If the object
of an act is incapable of being ordered to God—that is, if
the object contradicts the objective good of the person and
goods morally relevant to him—then the action is bad no
matter how good the intention and outcomes are. John Paul
II teaches, "There are objects of the human act which are by

their nature 'incapable of being ordered' to God, because they radically contradict the good of the person made in his image. These are the acts which, in the Church's moral tradition, have been termed 'intrinsically evil': they are such *always and per se*, in other words, on account of their very object, and quite apart from the ulterior intentions of the one acting and the circumstances."

Aquinas recognizes that there are some acts "that have deformity inseparably united to them, such as fornication, adultery, and others like them, which are in no way able to become good." He explains, "A good intention is not enough . . . it often happens that someone acts with a good intention, but fruitlessly, because he lacks a good will. Such is when someone steals in order to feed the poor: there is something of a good intention, but he lacks the necessary uprightness of the will. Consequently, no evil done with a good intention is excused." In the words of St. Paul, "And why not do evil that good may come?—as some people slanderously charge us with saying. Their condemnation is just" (Rm 3:8). Nor does an act's goodness derive primarily from some circumstance, such as the victim's age, racial heritage, or health status, or the manner in which an act is performed. Circumstances are merely additional qualities added to the substance of the act. They do not constitute the essence of the act any more than a person's height or hair color define him as a person.

What are some of the intrinsically evil acts, acts which are always sins? Christ's unequivocal condemnation of certain acts is a good place to start: "For out of the heart come evil thoughts, murder, adultery, fornication, theft, false witness, slander. These are what defile a man" (Mt 15:19–20). St. Paul also made an incomplete list of acts that are always sinful, saying, "Do you not know that the unrighteous will not inherit the kingdom of God? Do not be deceived; neither the immoral, nor idolaters, nor adulterers, nor homosexuals, nor thieves, nor the greedy, nor drunkards, nor revilers, nor robbers will inherit the kingdom of God" (1 Cor 6:9–10). John Paul II added genocide, abortion, euthanasia, suicide, mutilation, prostitution, contraception, slavery, unjust imprisonment, and defrauding a worker of his just wage. These are always unworthy of the human person and cannot actually be incorporated into union with God and life on its way to heaven. Consequently, such acts are morally prohibited for all people, all cultures, all political regimes, all times, without exception.

In the seventeenth century, Pascal mocked the moral doctrines of certain Jesuits who rejected objective standards and reduced goodness to intention. In a fictional dialogue, a Jesuit priest goes into raptures about how his Company can win over nominal Catholics by telling them that nearly any deed can be "purified" by directing one's intention to a good end while performing it. In this way, stabbing an enemy in the back after having been reconciled to him, giving money to someone to become a bishop, and assisting in a rape could be made good merely by having a good intention: "Not that we fail to deter men as far as we can from forbidden things, but when we cannot prevent the action, at least we purify the intention; and thus we correct the viciousness of the means by the purity of the end."

Pascal's pointed pen illustrated what John Paul II insisted on: we cannot understand biblical morality, the commandments, the covenants, or the virtues without recognizing that the object of an act is the source of morality. This is because we come to a rational and objective understanding of morality only by recognizing that the object of an act makes an act *what it is*, without a consideration of further intentions or circumstances. If the goodness of acts were measured without consideration of their objective nature, it would be impossible to affirm the existence of any objective moral order, or to establish any particular rule that would be universally binding. Consequently, morality would rest upon preference and power to the detriment of countless souls, the common good, and truth itself. The object of an act, therefore, is the decisive factor for morality. However, for an act to be good, the intentions and the circumstances must also be appropriate. As the principle goes, good is a conjunction of all good factors, whereas evil comes from any defect whatsoever.

In addition to distinguishing sins as either intrinsically evil or non-intrinsically evil (e.g., evil because of bad intention and/or because of circumstances), sins can also be distinguished as either mortal or venial. This distinction can be found in 1 John 5:17: "All wrongdoing is sin, but there is sin which is not mortal." Sin is a sort of chosen "sickness of the soul": some sins are like sicknesses that kill, and these are mortal; other sins are like sicknesses that merely weaken, and these are called "venial." Mortal sins entail death of the soul because they separate the soul from its principle of spiritual life, a life in accord with virtue ordered to the final end of union with God. A mortal sin thus is an act that violates virtue in a serious way, or goes against our final end, or destroys union with God, or all of the above. The soul then experiences a spiritual death, and its life cannot be restored without the direct intervention of God.

In contrast, venial sins are not "unto death." In the words of Aquinas, "He who sins venially neither does what the law forbids, nor omits what the law prescribes to be done, but he acts *aside* from the law because he does not observe the reasonable way of acting, which the law intends." If the soul, made in the image of God, is compared to an expert painting, mortal sin is like destroying the work, whereas venial sin is like defacing it. If life is compared to a journey, mortal sin is turning back from our final destination, whereas venial sin is stumbling or pausing along the way.

Augustine cogently argues that it is absurd and even insane to say that all sins are the same, just as it would be to say that a mouse and an elephant are the same because they are land animals, or that a mosquito and an eagle are equal simply because they both fly. A venial sin neither separates a soul from its life-principle nor excludes a person from the kingdom of God nor destines a person to eternal punishment, but it does merit temporal punishments as expiation. Hence, St. Paul says, "If any one builds on the foundation with gold, silver, precious stones, wood, hay, stubble—each man's work will become manifest; for the Day [of Judgment] will disclose it, because it will be revealed with fire, and the fire will test what sort of work each one has done. . . . If any man's work is burned up, he will suffer loss, though he himself will be saved, but only as through fire" (1 Cor 3:12–13,

15). Wood, which is more difficult to burn, represents the hardness of more significant venial sins which are difficult to remove from the soul; hay, which burns more quickly, represents lesser venial sins; and stubble, which is the chaff or husk of grain, is burnt in a flash like the lightest venial sins which are quickly purified in purgatory.

Aquinas argues that the objective nature of reality means that we ought to fear the final judgment, for God, the supreme judge, knows all things including our thoughts and words and deeds. Aquinas elaborates, "Now is the time of mercy; but the future time will solely be the time of justice. Hence, now is our time, but later will only be God's time." One of the many visions of St. Brigid of Sweden about God's judgment of souls may serve to drive home the message. She said that in a vision, she saw the soul of a young woman brought before the divine judge and his assisting host. The book of justice spoke about the young woman, saying that she had gone to confession for her sins, but she repented only slightly and had only weak contrition.

> Then the King said to the soul: "Let your conscience now declare those sins that were not accompanied by a proportionate satisfaction." Then the soul raised her voice. . . . She said: "Woe is me that I did not act according to God's commands, which I heard and knew!" Then she added in self-accusation: "I did not fear God's judgment." The book replied to her: "You must therefore now fear the devil." Right away the soul began to fear and tremble, as if she were melting away completely, and she said: "I had almost no love for

God: That is why I did so little good." An immediate
reply was made to her from the book [of judgment]:
"That is why it is just for you to approach closer to the
devil than to God."

Notice how it is the individual who judges herself and the
punishments correspond exactly to the sins. The account
continues:

> The soul said: "From head to heel there was nothing I
> did not dress with pride. Some of my vain and proud
> manners I invented myself. . . . I washed my hands and
> face not only to be clean but also to be called beautiful
> by men." A reply was made from the book: "Justice
> says it is the devil's right to repay you for what you
> have earned, since you dressed and adorned yourself
> as he inspired and told you to do." . . . The soul said:
> "I enjoyed it immensely when many people took after
> my example and noticed what I did and copied my
> manners." A reply was made from the book: "Hence,
> it is just that everyone caught in the sin for which you
> are about to be punished should also suffer the same
> punishment and be brought to you. Then your pain
> will be increased each time someone comes who cop-
> ied your fashions."

As a result of the judgment, the young woman then begins
to endure terrible torments, until her guardian angel cries
out. He reminds God that on her death bed the woman had
wanted to make true reparation for her sins and to love God
and avoid offending him. Such thoughts do not deserve hell.

In response, the Judge declared that because of his passion on the cross, she would be saved from eternal torments but must endure purgatory until she is purified.

It is worth noting that the guardian angel made an additional plea in favor of the young woman. He argued that she was too young to have a fully-developed conscience, by which we can infer that she was consequently not infected with fully-developed vice. Combined with the fact that she did repent to some degree, we can infer that she suffered from the condition of incontinence, which we will now analyze.

(4) Incontinence and (5) Vice

In the end, each of us chooses only one of "two ways": the way that leads to life or that which leads to death, the road of virtue or that of vice, the upward narrow path of good or the downward wide path of evil. Because these contrary ends are rather stable, we can recognize who belongs to them: the saints in heaven with everlasting virtue, the damned in hell with irreparable vice; the angels with God, the demons with Satan.

Most of us in this life, however, do not seem to fit comfortably in either category. Most of our actions do not reveal deeply established vice or the heights of virtue. A Stalin is rare, but so is a Mother Teresa. For the most part, we seem to fit somewhere in between. Aristotle helps explain why this is the case. His theory of "continence" and "incontinence" accounts for the meaningful psychological and behavioral differences between those who are *on the way* to some quasi-permanent habitual state and those who have "arrived" at the heights of virtue or the depths of vice. A single mortal sin is sufficient to send someone to hell, but it is not equivalent to vice. Sin is an act, whereas vice is a habit. As an acquired habit, vice gradually develops in the soul; like a seed of a poisonous plant, it grows over time, through the stages of its own organic development. Many acts make for a vice. When many acts incline a person to sin again, but the inclination is not a fully-blown habit of wickedness, a person is in the state of incontinence.

Just as virtue is the contrary to vice, so continence is the contrary to incontinence. Seeing their mutual connections, it may be easiest to consider them in relation to each other. The chart below describes the four different states of soul and their characteristic acts.

	Vice	Incontinence	Continence	Virtue
Kind of habit	Strong evil habits	Weak evil habits	Weak good habits	Strong good habits
Character- istics	Sin is easy and delightful	Sin comes often, but with sadness	Good is possible but difficult	Good is easy and delightful

Because a habit is the development of a power with respect to some object, the way individuals respond to a similar situation indicates the underlying state of soul. In what follows, I will explain each state of soul in light of one of the most fundamental issues to which a person can respond—namely, innocent human life.

To the far right is *virtue*, the stable, habitual perfection of a power directed toward the right end, which is ultimately union with God. A fully virtuous person has been victorious over his unruly passions to such a degree that he experiences at least volitional joy in doing the good. A high level of virtue may be seen in the example of Jérôme Lejeune, a French geneticist and physician who discovered the chromosomal malfunction that leads to Down syndrome. Contrary to Lejeune's desires, doctors used his studies to recommend aborting children with Down syndrome. In 1969, the American Society of Human Genetics awarded him for his research. In his acceptance speech, Lejeune courageously spoke against abortion and in favor of preserving the dignity of every life. From that point forward, his career was marked by a willingness to fight to protect unborn life and by the hostility his position drew. He exhibited great love for his neighbor and an extraordinary fortitude in the decades he spent giving talks, establishing foundations, writing materials, and working in a myriad of ways to protect the unborn. The cause to have the Catholic Church recognize him for heroic virtue is now underway.

Moving leftward—away from the good but still oriented toward it—continence is the state of a person who still struggles with untamed passions that are not yet fully subject to his right reason. A continent person does not have the fullness of virtue whereby doing good comes easily, quickly, and creatively in practically all exterior situations, whether he feels ill or well, tired or energized. A continent person does the right thing *for the most part* but with some mixture of difficulty, strain, and blandness because following reason does not feel right even though he knows it is. To use a medical analogy, a person in good health practically never feels an urge to "let go" of his bowels unexpectedly, and a virtuous person rarely, if ever, feels any movement to mess himself with an ignoble, base, sinful action. In contrast, the continent person feels the strain of the compulsion to perform a disordered act but typically keeps himself from doing it.

Continence may be represented by the many good medical care providers who avoid providing abortions but perhaps feel some urge to perform them. Much pressure is exerted on pro-life nurses and doctors to capitulate, including the social pressure of being potentially rejected by their peers and the financial pressure of risking one's employment because of opposition to abortion. Silence could be entirely virtuous in such conditions. St. Thomas More virtuously remained silent for as long as he could. But if silence is maintained for lesser motives, then it may represent a good habit that falls short of heroism, or even of virtue itself.

Next is incontinence, a state of disorder. From a medical point of view, an "incontinent" person is unable to maintain voluntary control over execratory functions. Such a person cannot contain their internal waste and can experience embarrassing moments of messing themselves. This is an accurate, if distasteful, image of the morally incontinent person unable to maintain control of his disordered impulses. When presented with some pleasurable object, the incontinent man knows he should not pursue it, but when he feels a rush of desire, he goes after it anyway—as a person might feel impelled to buy something despite his better judgment. Moral *incontinence* can be defined as "a condition that is present when a man has a correct evaluation of what he ought to do or avoid but draws away to the contrary by reason of the passion of desire." It should be noted that a person might be inclined away from reason because of an innate biochemical imbalance, or from sickness, or something of that sort. These dispositions also can be considered forms of incontinence, but here we are concerned with how personal choice leads to the incontinent state. Usually, a person is incontinent in only one realm or another: perhaps a person does not control sudden movements of desire for alcohol or sweets but can check his anger and curiosity.

Incontinence can be represented by doctors in Ireland who have performed abortions for the first time. A qualitative study found that at least half of the fetal medical specialists experienced "psychological burden" upon performing abortions and "described feticide as 'brutal', 'awful' and 'emotionally difficult', referring to it as 'stabbing the baby in the heart', and held themselves responsible for the death of the baby: 'I caused the death.'" Some physicians seem to be wavering between incontinence and vice. One reports his experience of performing many abortions: "It is always very sad and emotional, it is difficult but something that I guess I have been doing for a long time and I am aware that I am doing it for a long time. It doesn't necessarily mean it is easier, it is always very sad." Another says, "I remember getting sick out in the corridors afterwards because I thought it (feticide) was such an awful procedure and so dreadful. You have to see the positive in it otherwise you would drive yourself mad."

To the far left of the chart there is the state of vice. If a person has continually and deliberately performed many evil acts, having chosen contrary to what reason recommends and continually taken the bait of pleasure, his soul will become corrupted in a quasi-permanent way. *Vice* is a state in which one's reason is dominated by strong perverse desires to such a degree that reason pursues the end presented to it by the perverse desires. The result is that a person with vice "will perform evil actions by choice." Deep-seated bad habits of vice eventually encompass the whole person so that he characteristically pursues whatever is pleasing to him: he "superabounds in seeking pleasures," and he does not regret luxuriating in them. Indeed, a vicious person is often an "expert" in perpetrating his most precious evil deeds, whether in extorting money as a mafia boss, lying with faux friendliness as a high-ranking politician, discovering ever new ways to become drunk, and so on.

Vice might be represented by the physician Kermit Gosnell, who murdered numerous babies born alive in his horrific blood-spattered clinic, destroyed and falsified records, instructed untrained staff to perform delicate medical procedures, and gravely injured many women through grossly negligent treatment such as puncturing a uterus. Prior to his conviction, Gosnell said he thought he would be vindicated as a good man and a competent doctor. Such a self-assured declaration is a classic sign of advanced vice, indicating that he was so immersed in lies that he was convinced of the righteousness of his cause, or that he believed a few more lies could save him, or both. His jury disagreed.

How does a person develop appalling vice? Norman Doidge explains the physiological underpinnings of such behavior. The brain's adaptability, or plasticity, enables a person to develop all sorts of habits—even the most despicable and perverse—until the indulgence of those habits feels natural and satisfying. The chemical dopamine plays a key role in a reward feedback loop: when we achieve some difficult good, our brain releases dopamine, which gives us a sense of achievement and energized pleasure. When you get the sought-for job, dopamine is released; your coworker who did not get the job gets no dopamine. For naturally rewarding activities, such as eating sugary and fatty foods or interacting with loved ones, the reward system works quickly and efficiently to create an attachment to those goods. But even non-naturally rewarding objects or activities can become associated with pleasure.

The mind's ability to consider events and objects from different angles, and see a good side to something that is ordinarily repugnant, entails that a person can learn to find pleasure in almost anything. Utilizing language that Aquinas would recognize, Doidge explains that sufficiently gratifying rewards activate the "appetitive pleasure system," which governs dopamine delivery and wires the brain to desire what gave it a sense of satisfying pleasure. As noted by one of the "incontinent" doctors above, one can learn to "be positive" about performing the act of sticking scissors into the heart of an infant. The additional monetary and social rewards help reinforce the dopamine hit that one feels upon successful performances, even of abortion. When the action is repeated often enough and the rewards are delivered in adequate doses—one's extra cash increases with each abortion, one's career moves forward the more one is seen to be part of "the club"—then waves of nausea can be replaced by a sense of professional satisfaction, even pride, in doing the job efficiently. Hence, any habitual behavior, even killing innocent and helpless babies, can be described in terms of an "acquired taste" in which a habit loop of reward creates delight at some stimulus.

Significantly, many rewarding activities can permanently change the dopamine delivery system. Studies have shown that addictions to drugs such as cocaine and habitual activities such as running accumulate a dopamine-activating chemical in the brain with nearly irreversible change. The result is a stable system of habit-driven behavior. Although we might learn and make new habits, some of the deepest, oldest, and most powerful habits maintain roots in the deep crevices of our psyche. This may help explain the grip that vice can have on the soul. As one author has said, "Vice . . . adheres so pertinaciously to habit that it even cuts off nature from itself. . . . Vice is the proof of infamy and the sign of disgrace which repels affections from any fellowship with what is noble, that is, zealous and perfective of man. . . . Vice is a chain and a fetter, binding the soul in the prison of earthly things. . . . Vice is a dreadful tyrant which steals away our liberty and enslaves us."

(6) Despair or Presumption

When thoughts, words, and deeds are directed by a single end, they belong to a single species of sin. Aquinas illustrates,

"The angry man, through desire of vengeance, is at first disturbed in thought, then he breaks out into words of abuse, and lastly he goes on to wrongful deeds." When these three operations are coordinated regularly, they establish the state of incontinence with respect to the object of the sin (e.g., restraining anger), and when they are repeated sufficiently, they crystallize the state of vice. Despair and presumption follow next and naturally "just as boyhood and youth follow the complete generation of a man." Gregory the Great explains, "When the sin has once begun to issue into habit, then, alas! The sinner feeds himself either with the fallacious hope of God's mercy, or with the open and recklessness of despair . . . insofar as he either extravagantly colors to himself the mercifulness of his Maker, or is extravagantly terrified at the sin that he has done." Gregory then gives voice to the sinner's lament: "Even after the open act of sin, why, yet further, did the custom too take me up in it, to make me stronger to commit sin, and to nurse and sustain me with habitual wicked acts? After I entered into the habit of sin, why did I rear myself to a more tremendous pitch of iniquity, either by reliance on false hope, or by the milk of a miserable despair?"

If the soul does not despair, then the mind, being bound by so many chains of habitual evil, feels sapped of strength; "when it has no power to get free, [it] turns to some resource or other of fallacious consolation"; namely, it flatters itself that God is so merciful that he will not cast it into hell.

As an emotion, despair is "the privation of hope, a withdrawal from a desired thing because of an estimation that it is impossible to obtain." Sometimes, when a sinner considers the reachability of God, he might despair out of fear of God's infinitely just wrath. Other times, the horror of one's own sin unmasks the infinite distance between oneself and God. The sinner then wrongly believes that God refuses to pardon a repentant sinner or that God will not transform a sinner interiorly by grace. The false conclusion is that the sinner is necessarily damned, eternally captured by evil.

Aquinas astutely pinpoints the connection between self-satisfaction, hedonism, and despair. He argues that despair is primarily caused by *acedia*—that is, sadness at the difficulties incumbent upon reaching the good. That gloomy, listless vice leads to spiritual lethargy and a consequent despair that obstacles will forever prevent the soul from reaching God. Acedia in this sense is a sort of egocentrism that does not want to extend itself to difficult things but instead retreats in on itself to avoid pain.

Secondarily, despair is bound to hedonism within a vicious habit loop. When a person is sufficiently infected with a love of bodily pleasures, among which sexual pleasures and drugs are most powerful, then this disordered love "leads man to have a distaste for spiritual things, and not to hope for them as arduous goods." So hedonism causes despair. But despair also causes hedonism because "when hope is given up, men rush headlong into sin, and are drawn away from good works." Hedonism born of despair became prominent in nineteenth-century Europe when the mental lives of Christians became "horizontalized" and they no longer anticipated a heavenly future but instead settled for mundane pleasures. Even petty revels seem dear once the world becomes devoid of transcendent goals, as depicted in

Orwell's *Nineteen Eighty-Four* and in Huxley's *Brave New World*. In Orwell's vision, fornication seems to provide the main character a foundation to real meaning in an otherwise grey world of lies; in Huxley's version, the state maintains power by placating the masses with drugs, sex, and immersive entertainment.

Presumption is the other final result of chosen evil. Whereas despair expresses hopelessness, presumption offers false hope. Some sinners presume that they can get to heaven by their own power, even without living for God: "I'm a good person, aren't I? I haven't murdered anyone; I don't steal; I respect the environment." Others presume against the Holy Spirit, the principle of holiness, because they desire some good from God, such as salvation, without righteousness or repentance, or they desire the glories of heaven without supernatural merit. One of the gravest sorts of presumption is when God's ministers suppose that God will bring good to them no matter what evil they commit. Such was denounced through the prophet Micah:

> [Zion's] heads give judgment for a bribe,
>   its priests teach for hire,
>   its prophets divine for money;
> yet they lean upon the Lord and say,
>   "Is not the Lord in the midst of us?
>   No evil shall come upon us."
> Therefore because of you
>   Zion shall be plowed as a field;
> Jerusalem shall become a heap of ruins,
>   and the mountain of the house a wooded height.
>   (Mi 3:11–12)

The presumptuous person supposes that God does not care how men live, so long as they have at least some good intention. Aquinas calls this sort of presumption "despising the assistance of the Holy Spirit" and desiring contradictories—for it presumes to possess the holiness of heaven while remaining in sin and the rewards of virtue without directing oneself to God above all. It is a very grave sin, he says, because it counts on God's power for something unfitting to God. Furthermore, this sort of presumption arrogantly supposes that it knows the true nature of mercy and justice better than God himself, for it contradicts Sacred Scripture, which states, "Because he has despised the word of the LORD, and has broken his commandment, that person shall be utterly cut off; his iniquity shall be upon him" (Nm 15:31). Presumption also contradicts Christ, who did not deny the consequences of sin but rather came to save people from sin by uniting salvation to repentance and true faith: "Jesus came into Galilee, preaching the gospel of God, and saying, 'The time is fulfilled, and the kingdom of God is at hand; repent, and believe in the Gospel'" (Mk 1:14–15).

Climbing Out of the Pit

Just as one can identify the stages of cancer growth, so one can identify the stages of evil's increasing corruption. This chapter has been devoted to discussing how evil habits spiral downward. It is a slippery slope, but there is no inevitability to sin. At any point before death, God's grace can intervene, and a person can choose to say, "I stop here. I shall slide no more." He might have wicked thoughts and avoid expressing them in speech; he might say evil things but avoid putting them into practice; he might commit a single sin but only once; he might experience incontinence and not develop the ease of vice; and he might have vice but repent before he develops despair or presumption. The stages are organically united, but just as one's growth can be stunted, so one's sins can fall short of full maturation.

A wonderful example of climbing out of the pit of evil is St. Augustine. In his classic autobiographical work the *Confessions*, he describes how he experienced the four different states of habits: vice, incontinence, continence, and virtue. His gradual progress in virtue teaches us to take heart: no matter what stage of vice or virtue we might occupy, heroic habits are always possible.

Augustine attests that his early life was one marked by vice. As a teenager, for instance, he stole pears and threw them away for no apparent reason; later, he unashamedly took various mistresses; and he pursued fame and honor as a rhetorician. During this period of deeply engrained bad habits, he says, "I was wretched, and every soul is wretched that is bound in affection of mortal things: it is tormented to lose them, and in their loss becomes aware of the wretchedness which in reality it had even before it lost them. . . . I raged and wept in torment, unable to rest, unable to think. I bore my soul all broken and bleeding and loathing to be borne by me; and I could find nowhere to set it down to rest."

After wandering spiritually and physically, Augustine made his way from one heresy to another and started to recognize the good. In his state of incontinence, he no longer was entirely blinded by evil, but he was not yet ready to give up his sins. He writes to God, "I in my great worth-lessness—for it was greater thus early—had begged You for chastity, saying: 'Grant me chastity and continence, but not yet.' For I was afraid that You would hear my prayer too soon, and too soon would heal me from the disease of lust which I wanted satisfied rather than extinguished."

God did not leave Augustine in that bad state for long. Augustine states that as he grew closer to God, his prayer for virtue became, "Let it be now, let it be now." At this new stage, he still fell into sin on occasion, but he did not fall as far as he previously had been. No longer did his vices oppose him face to face. Instead, they softly muttered behind his back. Still, he remained hesitant about leaving his vices behind entirely. He reports, "The strong force of habit said to me, 'Do you think you can live without them?" But the hook had been pulled out of his soul. He writes:

> In the direction towards which I had turned my face and was quivering in fear of going, I could see the austere beauty of Continence, serene and indeed joy-ous but not evilly, honorably soliciting me to come to her and not longer, stretching forth loving hands to receive and embrace me, hands full of multitudes of good examples. With her I saw such hosts of young men and maidens, a multitude of youth of every age, gray widows and women grown old in virginity, and in them all Continence herself, not barren, but the fruitful mother of children, her joys, by You, Lord, her Spouse. And she smiled upon me and her smile gave courage as if she were saying, "Can you not do what

these men have done, what these women have done?
Or could men or women have done such in themselves, and not in the Lord their God? The Lord their
God gave me to them. Why do you stand upon yourself and so not stand at all? Cast yourself upon Him
and be not afraid; He will not draw away and let you
fall. Cast yourself without fear, He will receive you and
heal you."

This scene, too often forgotten in those who remember
the life of Augustine, stunningly illustrates the state of goodness that has not yet achieved full virtue.

Soon thereafter, Augustine underwent a complete conversion. A child's voice said, "*Tolle, lege*," "Take and read," and
he took up and read St. Paul's letter to the Romans: "Let us
conduct ourselves becomingly as in the day, not in reveling
and drunkenness, not in debauchery and licentiousness, not
in quarreling and jealousy. But put on the Lord Jesus Christ,
and make no provision for the flesh, to gratify its desires"
(Rom 13:13–14). Then God gave Augustine a greater grace,
as he said to God, "By Your gift I had come totally not to
will what I willed but to will what You willed." He came to
realize interiorly that "by continence we are collected and
bound up into unity within ourself, whereas we had been
scattered abroad in multiplicity." His prayer became "O
Charity, my God, enkindle me! You command continence:
give what You command, and command what you will."
Augustine went from strength to strength and from grace to
grace, until he achieved heroic virtue before death.

CHAPTER 7

HABITS FOR LIFE

Though he had entered his eighty-fourth year, St. Martin of Tours did not slacken in his activity. The weakness of age did not diminish the ardor of his zeal. Despite knowing in advance the coming of his death, the bishop and monk nevertheless traveled to a remote part of his diocese to reconcile quarrelling clergy. Having accomplished this task, arguably more difficult than saving a city from barbarians, he told his disciples that his time had come to pass on to the next life. With tears and earnest pleadings, they begged him not to abandon them. Although he was ready to leave this world behind, St. Martin was moved. He therefore prayed, "Lord if I can still be useful to your people, I do not at all refuse the work; may Your will be done." Soon thereafter, God took Martin to himself.

As long as we live, more work awaits us in God's vineyard, and while we draw breath, we can always grow in holiness.

In previous chapters, I have laid out the nature of habits; models for understanding and developing them; how they exist in our emotions, mind, and will; what truly constitutes heroic habits; and the downward spiral of evil habits. In this final chapter, I shall describe how the habitual readiness to flourish is the key to having good habits in this life, and for eternity in heaven. In this way, we can persevere to end like St. Martin and fulfill the Psalm:

> The righteous flourish like the palm tree,
>   and grow like a cedar in Lebanon.
> They are planted in the house of the LORD,
>   they flourish in the courts of our God.
> They still bring forth fruit in old age,
>   they are ever full of sap and green,
> to show that the LORD is upright. (Ps 92:12–15)

This chapter discusses, first, the habitual readiness to flourish, a habit that is necessary for the development of all other good habits; next, habitually disordered emotions, a key obstacle to fully flourishing; and finally, prayer, a key practice by which all other good habits may be obtained.

The Habitual Readiness to Flourish

There are two sorts of beings that cannot have habits: whatever is perfect and whatever is not alive. First, there is God. The one true God is always infinitely perfect in every way: he cannot grow, he cannot learn, he cannot become better, he cannot change, and he cannot develop habits. Any imperfection is impossible for the substantial and living perfection that is God himself. Second, there are nonliving things, including rocks, chairs, and corpses. These cannot develop habits, because they have no principle of improvement within themselves. They can only crumble, break, and decay. All living creatures, however, *can* develop habits. Indeed, to be perfect, we humans *must* develop habits, for when one of our powers is perfected, it is perfected through a habit.

All of us start life with raw unformed potential. A habit is the shape our raw potential takes after it has been chiseled through experience and choice. A good habit is a perfection of a power; a bad habit is a corruption of a power. Bad habits, as we have seen, gnaw at us to submit ourselves to them and follow the spiral downward to our ultimate destruction. Evil habits weaken us and make us more liable to failure and sadness. In contrast, good habits are dynamic principles that urge us to perform acts that will perfect ourselves and our world in a virtuous cycle, a perfective habit loop. The right habits make us more powerful by focusing and directing our potential, similar to how light becomes more powerful when it is focused and directed as a laser. Good habits therefore prepare us to engage the difficulties of the world and to overcome them with creativity and joy.

Flourishing is one way to characterize the state in which our habits have reached mature growth within us and are manifested in our lives. The force and dynamism of a thing's form—its nature—expresses itself by unfolding its material elements through time. For a plant, flourishing is the result of its effort in driving down its roots, extending its trunk, enduring varying weather conditions, and sprouting forth leaves in accordance with its nature. A sign of a healthy, robust plant is its flourishing, and the sign of lack of health is a failure to thrive. When our souls are in a spiritually healthy state and united to God through habits that accord with our nature, who is the source of all life, we flourish.

Sacred Scripture often utilizes the analogy of flourishing
to describe a person whose habits have reached a certain perfection. The very first Psalm compares the righteous man
to a flourishing tree and the unrighteous to chaff or dust.
Through the second nature given us by sanctifying grace,
which abides in a habitual way in the heart of our soul, we
can then flourish supernaturally. Summarized in the chart
are the stark contrasts Aquinas noted, which exist between
a person who participates in God's own divine life and one
who, through sin, has no such principle of flourishing.

	Nature	Righteous	Unrighteous
Planting	Plants need their roots to receive water.	Human nature becomes rooted in God to receive grace.	Evil men are rooted in and sustained by exterior things.
Bearing fruit	Healthy plants bear fruit.	The righteous manifest the fruits of the Holy Spirit (see Gal 5:22).	The wicked are without the water of grace, so their malice bears no spiritual fruit.
Conservation	Some trees have living bark but dead leaves, whereas others bear living leaves.	The good might have weak or dead works, but the righteous will not be deserted by God even in the smallest exterior works.	The wicked are driven about the earth by tribulations regarding superficial goods. "Those who plow iniquity and sow trouble reap the same" (Jb 4:8).

In another place, quoted in the opening of this chapter, the Psalms indicate that the righteous flourish like the
palm tree and grow like a cedar in Lebanon (Ps 92:12). St.
Robert Bellarmine interprets this to mean that just as the
palm grows straight and bears sweet fruit that lasts, so the

righteous develops in upright habits and bears the fruit of good works that have eternal benefits. As the cedars of Lebanon are exceedingly strong and tall, so the righteous reach the exceeding heights of virtue and remain extremely robust and firmly rooted in perseverance, which no wind of temptation can topple.

Developing the ancient Jewish imagery, Christ attests, "By this my Father is glorified, that you bear much fruit, and so prove to be my disciples. . . . You did not choose me, but I chose you and appointed you that you should go and bear fruit and that your fruit should abide" (Jn 15:8, 16). Commenting on this passage, Aquinas counts four fruits that a person will bear if he abides in Christ: he will avoid sin, be eager to accomplish works of holiness, be eager for the progress of others, and will produce fruit in eternal life, since "eternal life is the last and most perfect fruit of our labors." Augustine recognized a fifth: Christ himself is our fruit, for Christ is both the principle and origin of our spiritual life, and when we abide in Christ through charity, we bring him into the world through our love and good works.

Not all people are in the state of righteousness and full flourishing, or in the state of withering wickedness and aptness for punishment. As we saw in the last chapter, many, perhaps most, individuals are somewhere in between, occupying various shades of continence or incontinence. Here, too, the image of flourishing provides valuable insights. Plants in all stages of life, whether seedlings bearing first flowers or mature trunks seasoned with many fruit-bearing years, all retain the principle of life—and that entails continual development. Indeed, perpetual growth is a necessary factor in the life of any plant: lack of growth is a sign that it has begun to die, if is not already dead. Similarly, the person must always grow toward the good if it is to live. As the saying goes, "to not advance is to fall back."

The image of climbing a mountain or ladder is another classic image of habit growth. Pilgrims who walked the steep road up the slope of Mount Zion would sing what came to be known as the "gradual Psalms" or "songs of ascent" (Psalms 120–134). Their songs represented the soul's spiritual journey, in which there is no level middle ground: one is always either ascending the heights or descending to the depths. Just as it is easier to run down a mountain than to climb it, so the spiritual life takes more strength, effort, and focus. But rather than tiring out the pilgrim, as happens in physical journeys, each step of greater virtue increases one's spiritual strength, for each step prepares one for the next and brings one closer to heaven.

Human progress and growth exist primarily outside of the material realm. Plutarch reports that during Alexander the Great's youth, "whenever he heard [his father] Philip had taken any town of importance, or won any signal victory, instead of rejoicing at it altogether, he would tell his companions that his father would . . . leave him and them no opportunities of performing great and illustrious actions." Alexander was so keen to pursue glory through his own action that he preferred to have battles before him to win rather than riches in his hands. In the visible realm, one will eventually run into the limits of material resources, including one's native powers. It is the opposite in the realm of the spirit, where one can always become more virtuous, more perfect with grace. There is no limit to one's growth in charity in this life, as Aquinas says: "charity is normally in perpetual growth." Even more: as charity increases, it further augments one's capacity for increase in a truly exceptional growth pattern.

Through the strength of growing charity, all of a person's habits can grow and intensify: "They go from strength to strength" (Ps 84:7). In order for this to be possible, a person needs not only to focus on perfecting particular habits—strengthening his courage if he is cowardly, disciplining his temperance if he is dissolute, and so on—but also a more general habit that helps him to grow as needed. I call this a "habitual readiness to flourish." Part of this readiness is an openness to the timing decided by God and nature. In the present epoch, we expect instant results and impatiently await lengthy organic development. Consequently, we need to cultivate the patience of a farmer who knows that a crop will not weigh heavy with bounty overnight. He plants his seed, waters it, and waits for the fruit to come in due course.

A habitual readiness to flourish includes a willingness to change for one's own good. There are not a few people who refuse to adapt to the world as it truly is but instead become fixed in their ways and play in a constructed fantasy that approximates the world as they would like it to be. Lack of adaptation, of course, is only appropriate for what is most perfect (God) and for what is most imperfect. Inflexible persons sometimes think that they possess a quasi-divine understanding of the world and hardly consider that their attitudes may be closer to the state of an unintelligent rock. Undoubtedly, a person should not be willing to change in any way whatsoever—no one should be like Jell-O, which takes the form of any mold into which it is poured. No one should be prouder for compromising her morals more often, or for having an indecisive will that moves like a flag with the winds of popularity. But one should be open to authentic growth, to real flourishing, even when that means being pruned. "I am the true vine," Christ says, "and my Father is the vinedresser. Every branch of mine that bears no fruit, he takes away, and every branch that does bear fruit he prunes, that it may bear more fruit" (Jn 15:1–2).

Good Habits Feel Bad at First

If trees could move, they would squirm when being pruned. All things naturally try to avoid what they experience as painful. Hence, most pagans and Christians have this in common: when something feels unpleasant, they conclude that it is bad for them. Pagans might reason that whatever is unpleasant is not worth one's effort, or that one's time is better spent pursuing what is enjoyable. Christians might dress up this thinking with choir robes and argue that if something gives them a negative feeling, it is probably not from God. They "discern" that if warm fuzzies are absent, the Holy Spirit of consolation must be absent too.

I disagree. In what follows, I'll show that the contrary is far more often the case: for the great majority of people, at least at first, doing the *right thing* often entails *feeling badly* about it. Indeed, sometimes *feeling good* about an action is a sign of *deep vice*. The reason for this counterintuitive state of affairs is that our habits shape our judgments. To see how this is the case, we need to consider how we experience the exterior world and our interior states.

With our power of attention, we can focus our minds to consider some object outside of ourselves: a mouse on the ground, the hawk circling overhead waiting for a moment to strike. We can also consider our interior states: mental states including preoccupying thoughts, firm judgments, and vivid images in our imagination and memory; emotional states, such as a present joy at hearing from a friend, or a lingering mood related to brooding thoughts; and bodily states, such as discomfort in your back muscles, a rumbling gut, or light-headedness.

When we are occupied in paying attention to some exterior object, such as watching a video or listening to our favorite music, we might quickly toggle to consider our interior states and then return to the object at hand. If you notice that your foot is asleep, for example, you might adjust your posture. Often, however, our interior states go unnoticed by our conscious mind and are instead regulated by a complex subconscious system. Our senses operate quasi-independently, enabling us to perceive exterior objects, our bodily states, and our emotional states without deliberately adverting to them. Our estimative judgment takes stock of these perceptions and impels us to respond according to the direction established by previous choices and habit. Consequently, we have subconscious feelings and quasi-judgments, and we even perform some behaviors without fully knowing why. These partly voluntary behaviors can include commonplace behaviors, such as almost adjusting your posture or breathing, as well as more significant states, such as having an intuitional feeling and estimation that some situation or action "doesn't feel right," even if you cannot easily articulate reasons why.

Our subconscious intuitional system urges us to shy away from what feels odd, ill-fitting, uncomfortable, and unnatural, and instead to pursue what feels normal, appropriate for us, comfortable, and natural. Here, the power of our habits comes to the fore. Aristotle observes that deeply engrained habits become like a "second nature." While shaping one of our powers, habits also condition us to estimate that something in accordance with those habits is good, pleasant, and natural for us. Likewise, when something runs against our habits, we estimate it to be unpleasant, bad, and unnatural to us. As a result, one's disordered habits can lead to a "transvaluation of values" whereby a person perceives as bad what is good for him and feels that what is good is somehow bad.

Good habits feel bad at first.

We should never discount the possibility that our feelings may be distorted, especially as we work to develop the virtues that can become heroic habits. There is an analogy here with natural habits: to the obese, exercise is a terrible strain. But there is more. In the last chapter, we saw how sins of thoughts, words, and speech can lead to incontinence and vice. Accordingly, the seeming naturalness of wicked habits constitutes one of the main reasons why sin has such a powerful tug that pulls us down so easily.

Sin corrupts all of our faculties: it hatches ignorance in our reason, malice in our will, weakness in our assertive power, and disorder among our desires. In this state, vice feels increasingly like a beloved childhood blanket, whereas virtue feels awkward, unpleasant, and unintelligible. St. Paul teaches, "The unspiritual man does not receive the gifts of the Spirit of God, for they are folly to him, and he is not able to understand them because they are spiritually discerned" (1 Cor 2:14). Commenting on this passage, Aquinas explains that a person is called "unspiritual" because he is moved only by his lower appetites, not reason: "he follows the dissolute sensuality of his soul, which his rule of spirit does not keep within the measure of the order of nature." Without the Holy Spirit to inflame one's affections for spiritual goods and to become detached from sensible goods, the sensual person cannot grasp the meaning or purpose of spiritual goods, for as Aristotle said, "as a person is, so his end seems to him." We judge things through the lens of our character, which has been shaped by voluntary habits. Wallowing in the mud of the world, the piggish person is unable to look at the stars without dirt in his eyes: "a man given to sense cannot understand things that transcend sense, and a man attracted by carnal things does not realize that there are other goods besides those which please the senses."

Newman fully recognized that not everyone loves to worship God. Many of his sermons sound this theme: "Religion is in itself at first a weariness to the worldly mind." This is the case, Newman shows, for children, teens, adults, and even practicing Christians. Addressing himself to young people, Newman says about religion, "How irksome, cold, uninteresting, uninviting, does it at best appear to you! how severe its voice! how forbidding its aspect! With what animation, on the contrary, do you enter into the mere pursuits of time and the world!" To men of action, busy about things of the world, religion seems "weak and impotent." They seek entertainment, not prayer and union with God, for religion strikes them as ghastly, "a labour, it is a weariness, a greater weariness than the doing nothing at all." Many Christians in our day would be stung if they seriously considered Newman's observation that they *must* think that religion in itself is "dull and uninviting," for they always try to make it more exciting and add something to it which they find pleasurable, such as secular music and an emphasis on worldly success. If they were honest about their feelings, they would say:

> We will admit that we *ought* to be religious, and that, when we come to die, we shall be very glad to have led religious lives: but to tell us that it is a *pleasant* thing to be religious, this is too much: it is not true. . . . Religion is something unpleasant, gloomy, sad, and troublesome. It imposes a number of restraints on us; it keeps us from doing what we would; it will not let us have our own way; it abridges our liberty; it interferes with our enjoyments; it has fewer, far fewer, joys at present than a worldly life, though it gains for us more joys hereafter.

For Newman, a negative affective reaction to true religion indicates not a deficiency on the part of God but a defect on the part of the individual.

Like Aquinas and Newman, St. John of the Cross sees how repeated sin corrupts the various faculties. Whereas Aquinas only articulates the principles of how this operates and Newman provides a phenomenological description of the general psychological condition, the Carmelite gives a precise account of four degrees of harm caused by a person's withdrawal from God and disordered attachment to the world, which seems to represent the soul's downward slide from incontinence to vice.

First, a person experiences backsliding of the intellect. Just as a cloud darkens the air and prevents the sun from illuminating it, so sin corrupts the mind, darkening it through chaotic passion and obscuring the light of divine goods. John of the Cross writes, "By the very fact that spiritual persons . . . give reign to the appetite in frivolous things, their relationship with God is darkened and their intellect clouded." He quotes the book of Wisdom to explain: "For the fascination of wickedness obscures what is good, and roving desire perverts the innocent mind" (Ws 4:12). This creates a "dullness of mind" whereby holy things appear dull and the intellect develops a "darkness of judgment in understanding the truth [in general] and judging well of each thing as it is in itself." Not even a person's sanctity or learning will prevent this mental injury, John of the Cross observes, since disordered love for created things *by its very nature* attaches one's affections to those things and pulls the intellect along with it.

Second, the will spreads itself out to temporal things. In this situation, a person believes that joy and pleasure in creatures is a trifle and bears an unruffled conscience about disordered attachments. With this mentality, the soul unsurprisingly pursues a greater number of pleasures, and with greater intensity. The consequences of this state are "many kinds of serious harm," St. John observes, including: the soul withdraws from spiritual exercises and the things of God, it lacks satisfaction in these exercises because of the pleasure found in other things, and it gives oneself over to many imperfections, frivolities, joys, and vain pleasures. The key trait in this second stage, he says, "is extreme lukewarmness—as well as carelessness—in spiritual matters, observing them through mere formality, force, or habit, rather than through love." Such is a state very similar to what Aquinas describes as *acedia*, which, as we have seen, withdraws a person from spiritual things and leads him to become hedonistic. The Carmelite friar explains that the "consummation" of this stage consists in a person abandoning spiritual practices in general and instead fixing his mind and covetous desires on secular things.

Third, the soul completely abandons God. Without any concern whatsoever for God's law, persons in this state "attend to worldly goods and allow themselves to fall into mortal sins through covetousness." They become so forgetful and sluggish about the spiritual life that "in the affairs of God they are nothing, and in those of the world they are everything." They possess an unsatisfied and anxious desire for creaturely goods that nothing can satisfy: "Rather, their appetite and thirst increase more as they regress further from God," and they consequently fall into thousands of kinds of sins out their disordered love.

Fourth, the soul takes creatures as "gods" to which they offer the devotion of their intellect, will, and the rest of their faculties. As Aquinas said, "Whatever a person assigns to himself as an ultimate end in which his desire rests, can be called his god. Hence, when you have pleasure as end, pleasure is called your god, and the same for pleasures of the flesh and for honors." Even worse are the wicked who so subvert the right order of things that they subordinate "divine and supernatural things to temporal things as to gods." Simon Magus did thus when he thought of putting a price on God's grace by trying to buy it from St. Peter (see Acts 8:9–24). He wanted grace to increase his personal power and fame, and he tried to entice another to subordinate grace to a sense of greed.

St. John of the Cross says that many people are in this fourth stage, who serve money instead of God, making profit their ultimate end and god rather than the righteousness of the kingdom of Christ. Thus, too, are those who commit suicide because of some temporal loss, for they show that their lives were directed toward that good without which their lives had no purpose: since there was nothing to hope for from it, the person gives himself over to despair and death.

Our examination of the four stages of corruption of the soul, which extends from incontinence into the final corruption of vice and into despair, shows that persons in these states do not find joy in the things of God. They cannot, because they are so habituated to loving things apart from God that anything related to virtue, holiness, and fulfillment of God's holy will seems to them only pain and misery. Newman sharply observed:

> Heaven would be hell to an irreligious man. We know how unhappy we are apt to feel at present, when alone in the midst of strangers, or of men of different tastes and habits from ourselves. How miserable, for example, would it be to have to live in a foreign land, among a people whose faces we never saw before, and

whose language we could not learn. And this is but a faint illustration of the loneliness of a man of earthly dispositions and tastes, thrust into the society of saints and angels. How forlorn would he wander through the courts of heaven! He would find no one like himself; he would see in every direction the marks of God's holiness, and these would make him shudder.

Because of their deeply-habituated turn from God, people trekking their way down the mountain of God's law should not rely on their feelings to accurately measure the path of reality. Even those who are in the first stages of this downward trajectory from incontinence to vice, even Christians still practicing their religion to some degree, cannot see how death can lead to the resurrection. They see Christ nailed to the wood and think, "The cross for him, but not for me." The path of asceticism—with its sharp stones, thinner air, and a laborious climb with the sun in one's eyes—seems to promise only meaningless suffering. To such pilgrims, a sacrifice for virtue might *feel wrong*, and a comfortable vice might *feel right* and indeed the only reasonable thing to do. By sacrifice for virtue, I do not mean giving up time, money, or energy for any of a hundred actions that the world praises, such as rallying against global warming. I mean speaking up for the truth when one's job is at risk, or forgiving an enemy when revenge is within reach, or confessing one's sins to a mediocre priest—any of those actions require a sacrifice of "skin in the game" because of their abrasiveness.

Everyone frightened by the way of the cross, everyone who feels the pressure of virtue's chisel, everyone who experiences discouragement at his lack of progress, everyone who feels repulsed by the science of the saints should recall that heroic habits do not come quickly, cheaply, or without cost. Even St. Paul, who had already achieved a lofty level of virtue, could say, "For I delight in the law of God, in my inmost self, but I see in my members another law at war with the law of my mind and making me captive to the law of sin which dwells in my members" (Rom 7:22–23). Through his interior war, he became a great saint by fixing his mind and his will unswervingly on the heavenly crown of glory.

All of us who remain separated from heaven in this life should remind ourselves from time to time that because God is entirely good, to be united with him is the most delightful thing in itself, and one day, at least in the next life, we will experience that union as far more satisfying than any creature comfort. Drawing upon his own experience, Aquinas argues that spiritual pleasures "in themselves and absolutely speaking" are greater than sensory, bodily pleasures, for spiritual pleasures are greater, more beloved, more noble, more intimate, more perfect, and more lasting. John of the Cross similarly attested that people truly united with God receive untold advantages even in this life: "they acquire liberty of spirit, clarity of reason, rest, tranquility, peaceful confidence in God, and, in their will, the true cult and homage of God." Perhaps more surprisingly,

> they obtain more joy and recreation in creatures through the dispossession of them. . . . In detachment from things they acquire a clearer knowledge of them and a better understanding of both natural

and supernatural truths concerning them. Their joy, consequently, in these temporal goods is far different from the joy of one who is attached to them, and they receive great benefits and advantages from their joy. They delight in these goods according to the truth of them, but not those who are attached according to what is false in them; they delight in the best, whereas the attached delight in the worst; they delight in the substance of them, but those sensibly attached delight in the accidents.

Such we find in the saints, who were able to delight even in natural goods far more exuberantly than is possible aside from their union with God—as exemplified in St. Francis of Assisi's *Canticle of the Creatures* and the overabundant joyful description of natural phenomena in the Psalms. To take one phrase among many others:

> Let the heavens be glad, and let the earth rejoice;
>> let the sea roar, and all that fills it;
>> let the field exult, and everything in it!
> Then shall all the trees of the wood sing for joy
>> before the LORD, for he comes,
>> for he comes to judge the earth.
> He will judge the world with righteousness,
>> and the peoples with his truth. (Ps 96:11–13)

As Newman said, "The pleasures of sin are not to be compared in fulness and intensity to the pleasures of holy living. The pleasures of holiness are far more pleasant to the holy, than the pleasures of sin to the sinner." Therefore, no one should be surprised that he finds heroic habits distasteful, though they are so pleasant in themselves: "Men know what sin is, by experience. They do not know what holiness is; and they cannot obtain the knowledge of its secret pleasure, till they join themselves truly and heartily to Christ." To begin to "taste and see" the spiritual delights of union with God, one needs the regular practice of prayer, a habit that fittingly serves to complete this book.

The Habit of Prayer

There are few things as fascinating as watching another man work. Expertise attracts us. Excellence intrigues us. When we see an athlete perform at the top of his game, a carpenter carve through wood like butter, or a musician nonchalantly play a complex and moving piece, we almost naturally ask, "How do you do that?" This was the attitude of the disciples toward Jesus. After seeing him pray, they demanded, "Lord, teach us to pray" (Lk 11:1).

The disciples recognized Jesus as a master of the spiritual life. They had seen him heal the sick and cast out demons. They had heard him preach to crowds and explain divine mysteries. But they did not ask him to show them how to do any of these great things. What struck them more was how Jesus prayed. John Paul II points out, "Prayer was the life of his soul, and his whole life was prayer. Human history knows of no other personage who was so fully—and in such a way—absorbed in prayer with God, as was Jesus of Nazareth, Son of Man, and at the same time Son of God, 'one in Being with the Father'." They had witnessed the intensity and the love and the impact of his prayer, and this was so attractive that they wanted to develop those practices in their own lives. In this way, they demonstrated St. Paul's observation that "we do not know how to pray as we ought" (Rom 8:26) and Jesus's insistence that no one can come to the Father except through the Son (see Jn 14:6). Accordingly, Christ prayed that his disciples from thence forward might have an example of prayer and that we might join our prayers to his.

When I was a kid, my father once showed me a technique for testing the quality of a wooden instrument. He tapped a tuning fork and held it up to my ear. Its quiet note was faint but clear. While it was still vibrating, he put it onto the body of an acoustic guitar. The tone became louder and more robust: the guitar was well-made because it amplified the sound. Christ likewise sounds the note of prayer, and the nearer he comes to us, the more we share in his prayer, expressing it through our own person the way a guitar expresses the note given to it by the tuning fork. A Carmelite spiritual writer put it this way: "We cannot imagine a more intimate and profound prayer than the prayer of Jesus. . . . Only the prayer of Jesus is perfect praise and adoration of the Trinity, perfect thanksgiving and always efficacious supplication; He alone can offer infinite homage to the Trinity." It follows that "our prayer has value only insofar as we unite it to that of Jesus and try to make it an . . . extension of his." Augustine showed that such prayer is possible because of the Incarnation, whereby the Word of God, eternally united to the Father in godhead, was united to human nature: "When we speak to God asking mercy, we do not separate the Son from Him; and when the Body of the Son [the Church] prays, it does not separate the Head from itself, for it is one Savior of His Body, Our Lord Jesus Christ, the Son of God, who both prays for us, and prays in us, and is prayed to by us. He prays for us as our priest; he prays in us as our head; he is prayed to us as our God." Hence, like the disciples, we must ask Christ, "Jesus, pray *in* and *with* me to the Father as you pray to Him heart-to-heart."

Prayer can be defined as the raising up of the mind to God by charity. According to Aquinas, authentic prayer must be:

- *well ordered*, whereby spiritual goods are sought first, especially salvation, and secondarily temporal and material goods;
- *humble*, not presuming on one's own powers, but on divine goodness;
- *illuminated* by faith, which reveals things as they truly are;
- *confident*, persevering, and full of hope, so that one does not lose heart;
- *motivated* by devotion and charity, with love of God and neighbor;
- *suitable*, rightly asking for the true good;
- *attentive*, so that one never loses sight of the end for which one prays;
- and *communal*—that is, in harmony with the prayers of other devout souls—for "it is impossible for the prayers of the many not to be heard."

Two qualities sum up all of the qualities above; namely, prayer must be asked in the name of Jesus and ultimately ordered to the glory of the Father. As Christ teaches, "Whatever you ask in my name, I will do it, that the Father may be glorified in the Son" (Jn 14:13). Asking in Christ's name is equivalent to asking when we "abide" in him, for he says, "If you abide in me, and my words abide in you, ask whatever you will, and it shall be done for you" (Jn 15:7). Aquinas clarifies that Christ's promise here regards whatever we need for salvation.

Because Christ wants us to participate in his work of redemption, he commands us "always to pray and not lose heart" (Lk 18:1). Within the providential order of God, prayer is not a nice extra. It is indispensable. St. Alphonsus Liguori calls prayer the "necessary and certain means of obtaining salvation, and all the graces for salvation." To understand the great importance of prayer, we must respond to two errors about it: Activism and Quietism. Activism is the heresy of good works without prayer, and Quietism is the heresy of no works and some prayer.

Activism in this sense is a sort of Pelagian naturalism, which claims that we can initiate, and perhaps achieve, our own perfection without God's grace. A Christian Activist does not deny that God commands us to pray; he does not denigrate the power of grace; he will not claim that private prayer has no place in the life of an apostle. But he is not convinced that without grace, all our efforts are spiritually fruitless.

A practical Pelagian tends to think that when things are failing, we need better technology and a more efficient method. He has not yet fully grasped the meaning of Christ's declaration: "Apart from me you can do nothing. If a man does not abide in me, he is cast forth as a branch and withers" (Jn 15:5–6). A Pelagian might for a while pray precisely the prescribed amount and no more. But he will tend to neglect regular prayer and spiritual reading. Along with his activism comes a lowering of his horizons. Because he works with fervor, and is anxious to produce well, he starts to think that his intense activity excuses the lack of effort he puts into prayer. He will judge his success by exterior measures, not by spiritual growth. His fundamental error begins with the thought that he can accomplish a supernatural result with natural means, but he ends by overlooking the supernatural entirely.

Quietism, in contrast, is a sort of "ultra-supernaturalism." Instead of trusting in oneself to get everything done, Quietism supposes that God will do everything for us. Seeing the error of those who try to build a tower that will reach heaven, the Quietist commits his own error by deciding to do as little as possible. "Since Jesus won my salvation," he reasons, "I guess there's not much left for me to do." It's as if the chief virtue in Christian life is to get out of God's way. At first, this do-nothing attitude makes a person negligent in his duties. Perhaps a mother does spiritual reading for hours in order to avoid cleaning dishes, or a father goes to daily Mass but neglects to teach his children how to pray. Eventually, this way of thinking and acting—or not acting, as it were—has an ironic reversal: it leads the Quietist to pray less and less. He reasons, "If God is already taking care of everything, why do I need to get involved? I'll just mess things up." He confuses inactivity for resignation, carelessness for detachment, ignorance for faith, and presumption for trust. Sometimes the Quietist will go so far as to think that he should not pray for something because his own desire could obstruct God's plans. On the surface, Quietism may seem to be the path of holiness. Many people confuse quietism with piety. Pelagians are more obviously in error since they think they can do everything on their own. Nevertheless, Quietism has been condemned by the Church, for it denies that God can use creatures—including ourselves—as instruments of his grace.

When our Lord commands, "Do not be anxious about tomorrow," he condemns Activism (Mt 6:34). But when he rebukes the useless servant for squandering the talents entrusted to him, our Lord condemns Quietism (see Mt 25:14–30). Both errors do not comprehend that grace is the way God and man work together. Thomas explains that our perfection lies not only in allowing God to work on us but *especially* in cooperating with God's work through us. God is the primary agent. We are secondary agents, it is true, but no less agents for being secondary. We were not created to be passive, lifeless robots: we are, in St. Paul's terminology, "fellow workers" with God (1 Cor 3:9). Hence, Aquinas says, a supernatural effect, such as growth in faith or in charity, or becoming heroic in all our habits, is not attributed partly to us and partly to God. Rather, "it is done wholly by both, although in a different way," according to the power of our nature as transformed by grace.

Prayer is the chief means by which we cooperate with God. In Aquinas's words, "after baptism, man needs to pray continually, in order to enter heaven: for though sins are remitted through baptism, there still remain the traces of sin assailing us from within, and the world and the devils assailing us from without." Liguori builds upon this: "Without the divine assistance we cannot resist the might of so many and so powerful enemies," which tempt us to sin, "but this assistance is only granted to prayer; therefore without prayer there is no salvation."

When God commands us to pray, he does so because he wants to give us many gifts through prayer, and simultaneously, he wants to give gifts to others through our prayer. Prayer is the chief floodgate through which God gives us his power, so prayer must at least implicitly precede any action rooted in God. Our action is undeniably important, but the life, the supernatural power, the grace, the spiritual fruitfulness of our action begins in prayer.

Before Jesus began his public ministry, the Holy Spirit led him into the desert to pray; before Jesus chose his disciples, he spent the night in prayer; before he was crucified, he prayed in the upper room with his disciples and then in the Garden of Gethsemane. After Jesus's resurrection, this pattern was followed by the apostles: before they chose a successor to Judas, they prayed; before the Holy Spirit came and sent them to preach, they prayed with Mary; before they left on their missionary journeys and eventually to their martyrdom, they prayed. Prayer, therefore, constitutes the primary, the great, the necessary means of our salvation and heroism.

A life without prayer is like a tree without water. It might seem to be healthy at first, since it still has sap in its veins, but in a long and severe drought, first the leaves wilt, then the branches stiffen, then the very heart of the wood hardens and the roots dry up. The tree remains standing with its outward shape intact, but it is dead. It is only fit to be cut down and used for fire. Thus goes our soul when we deprive our souls of the life-giving water that is prayer.

We are now positioned to address why prayer is essential to the development of heroic habits.

Recall that a habit is a human perfection. Good habits perfect our various powers, making a particular action easier, quicker, more skillful, more fruitful, more delightful. Habits are necessary for our perfection. Habits are like the human hand. Some animals have claws, others have hoofs, still others talons. We humans have hands. The dexterity of hands makes them, in Aristotle's memorable phrase, "the tool of tools." Our hands are dexterous because our souls have the capacity to learn; learning in the soul is a habit that abides in the intellect. Consequently, just as the hand is a visible "tool of tools" by which we can accomplish our goals, so are habits "tools of the soul," for by them we are able to perform our exterior actions well. Whereas hands are natural tools given to us by the Creator through nature, habits are acquired "tools" that we develop in ourselves by means of repeated right practice. This is truest of the habit of prayer. St. Alphonsus insightfully observed, "I am certain that by prayer I shall obtain eternal life, and all the graces necessary to attain it; and . . . I know that God will not deny me the grace of actual prayer, if I will [it] (because he gives it to all men)." St. Thérèse of Lisieux describes the centrality and the great efficacy of prayer this way:

A scholar has said, "Give me a lever and a fulcrum, and I will lift the world." What Archimedes was not able to obtain, for his request was not directed by God and was only made from a material viewpoint, the saints have obtained in all its fullness. The Almighty has given them as fulcrum: Himself alone; as lever: prayer, which burns with a fire of love. And it is in this way that they have lifted up the world; and it is in this way that the saints still militant lift it, and that, until the end of time, the saints to come will lift it.

Hence, another spiritual writer aptly states, "Prayer is to the spiritual life, what the hand is to the body . . . as the hand does all things, so prayer does the same."

Prayer can be understood as habit in the sense of both a regular practice and a stable quality of the soul that unites us with God. When the disciples asked Jesus to teach them how to pray, they were recognizing that prayer is an art that can be taught and learned. Regular prayer practices that aid this habit acquisition include the Liturgy of the Hours, the Holy Rosary, and the Divine Mercy chaplet, as well as one- or two-second prayers that one can offer in the midst of one's work. These little prayers have been called "aspirations" because they are like sighs coming from our depths and moved by the Holy Spirit. They are also known as "arrow prayers" or "darts of fire" because they burn with our love and we shoot them up into the heart of God. The desert fathers recommended this practice, particularly in connection with the ancient and powerful Jesus Prayer: "Lord Jesus Christ, Son of the living God, have mercy on me a sinner."

Saints Jerome, Cassian, and Augustine all mention perpetual prayer, especially marking out short phrases sent up to heaven; St. Francis de Sales teaches it in his *Introduction to the Devout Life*, and St. Alphonsus Liguori gives us many examples of these prayers throughout his works. Through these various practices, applied regularly, attentively, and devoutly, a person develops the habit of prayer such that he is able to send up prayers to God easily and naturally, almost spontaneously as occasions arise.

These forms of exterior prayer can help us acquire a more stable habit of the soul, by which the intellect and will more stably and voicelessly commune with God. Aquinas describes this state as having one's intention unswervingly fixed on God. He notes that one can "pray continually" through "having a continual desire," in the sense that one's heart continually longs for union with God. The Carmelite friar Brother Lawrence of the Incarnation spoke of "the practice of the presence of God." St. Simeon the New Theologian explains what this means: "Do everything as though in the presence of God and so, in whatever you do, you need never allow your conscience to wound and denounce. . . . The mind should be in the heart. . . . It should guard the heart while it prays, revolve, remaining always within, and thence, from the depths of the heart, offer up prayers to God. When the mind, there, within the heart, at last tastes and sees that the Lord is good, and delights therein, then it will no longer wish to leave this place in the heart."

St. Simeon notes that this practice goes by many names: silence of the heart, attention, sobriety and opposition to evil thoughts, guarding the mind. The ancient monks would employ this practice of "guarding the heart, convinced that, through this practice, they would easily attain every other virtue, whereas without it not a single virtue can be firmly established." The key thing to remember in relation to this practice is that it is a habit enlivened by grace, which means that it takes effort and time to develop, but it can be learned. Eventually, the presence of God in the soul becomes a guest as familiar and welcome as we are to ourselves. Prayer then becomes a habit whereby all other habits are gained, purified, and directed to God: "When prayer takes possession of us," one spiritual writer says, "it gradually transforms us, and spiritualizes us as a result of our union with the Holy Spirit."

In conclusion, human perfection consists in good habits; the height of habits are heroic habits; among the greatest is the habit of prayer, for it aims at the greatest goods and makes us godlike. Prayer is a supreme habit for life. Prayer is for life because it is in favor of life—it *promotes* life, acquiring all the graces we need for salvation, sanctity, and even spiritual heroism. It is also for the lives of others, particularly their everlasting life in heaven. Finally, prayer is for *life* because it will remain with us forever. Those who pray on earth will become a prayer to God in heaven, joining the saints in their eternal hymn, "To him who sits upon the throne and to the Lamb be blessing and honor and glory and might for ever and ever!"

Epilogue

The next life will reveal the true nature of our habits. Dante saw the classic pagan heroes in the *Inferno*: Achilles, Hector, Aeneas, Caesar, and Ulysses. Compared to the heights of virtue to which we are all called, they were hardly heroes at all. The truest heroes are found in the *Paradiso*. There, for example, St. Bonaventure tells the tale of St. Dominic, "the amorous lover of the Christian faith, the holy athlete, gentle to his own and savage to his foes," a "laborer chosen by Christ to help Him dress and keep His garden" so that it might grow and blossom and bear "admirable fruit." Bonaventure explains his motives: "To sing the praises of so great a champion / the ardent courtesy and fitting discourse of Brother Thomas inspired me." Our look at heroic habits has been similarly inspired.

It is said that when Thomas Aquinas would walk past a field, peasants gaped at his large size. Now we might gaze admiringly at the greatness of his soul. Thomas remained unassuming throughout his life, even when praised by Albert the Great, one of the most learned men of the era, and when offered a bishopric or two. Thomas was untroubled by seeming ordinary. Although he strove for the highest perfection, he measured greatness as God does, not according to the standards of the world. He continually insisted that the good of grace in the soul is greater than the natural good of the whole universe and that perfection does not consist in some exterior act but rather in following Christ, which is done through charity.

Aquinas's greatness was not the fruit of a radical conversion from a sordid past, as was the case for Augustine, nor was it manifested in a sparkling personality that won crowds like Francis of Assisi. Nevertheless, he developed the greatest habits to a heroic degree, seen best in his love of wisdom and devotion to prayer. In an almost autobiographical passage, Aquinas explains:

> Let us suppose that a person has a candle that is covered. He would not look for another light, but to have that which he has uncovered. Thus, we do not have to look for wisdom anywhere but in Christ: *for I decided to know nothing among you except Jesus Christ and him crucified* (1 Cor 2:2). *When he appears*, that is, is revealed, *we shall be like him*, that is, knowing all things (1 John 3:2). In other words, if I had a book in which all knowledge was contained, I would seek to know only that book; similarly, it is not necessary for us to seek any further than Christ.

More than in study or books, Aquinas sought—and found—Christ through the habit of prayer. Those who knew him attested that while saying Mass, he was utterly absorbed by the sacramental mystery, and his face ran with tears. At night, he would rise after a short sleep and pray, lying prostrate on the ground. It was in those nights of prayer that he learned what he would write or dictate in the daytime.

Aquinas's rhythm of life was regulated by his orderly, God-centered habits grounded in a habitual readiness to flourish. Thomas allowed himself only a minimum of time for sleeping and eating, while all the rest was given to prayer, reading, thinking, writing, or dictating: "never an idle moment, always a holy activity." His private secretary, his friend, Brother Reginald, insisted that Thomas's vast knowledge *was not* the mere result of natural intelligence and hard work: those were necessary but insufficient causes. "All of Thomas's writing began with prayer," Brother Reginald noted, "and in all his difficulties he had recourse to prayer, with many tears; after which he never failed to find his mind cleared and his doubts resolved." The chief cause of Thomas's greatness was the chief cause of all heroism: the Holy Spirit, who fills the soul with charity and makes the highest form of prayer a habitual activity that makes it possible for everyone to have heroic habits. Thomas practiced these habits as a Dominican friar, but he had learned them in his childhood as a Benedictine oblate.

For those who want practical advice on how to develop heroic habits, I can do little better than to follow the example of St. Thomas and to take St. Benedict as my model and say: pray and work.

NOTES

Chapter 1

He hurriedly dipped his quill . . .
This narrative sequence encapsulates many integrated behaviors manifested in a well-developed habit. It will be valuable to re-read this portion after having completed the book to see how it integrates and describes later issues discussed more at length.

"Therefore, there can be such a disturbance of anger . . ."
From the *Summa Theologiae* [hereafter: ST], I-II, q. 48, a. 4, c. This question immediately proceeds the "Treatise on Habits," which begins in q. 49 after a brief prologue.

It was a fasting day.
Originally, Dominicans fasted from meat from September 14, the Feast of the Holy Cross, until Easter day. A fast day during that period meant even less food.

"Doesn't he ever get tired?"
Aquinas would often pray much of the night, and while he was working, he would go into a trance-like state, even to the point of forgetting to eat. This led to some humorous incidents, as when he became focused on the heretical Manichean sect while dining in the presence of the king of France. See the accounts of Bernard Gui, and others, in *The Life of Saint Thomas Aquinas: Biographical Documents*, trans. and ed. Kenelm Foster (London: Longmans, Green and Co., 1959), 44–45.

" . . . mark a new section . . ."
This is almost verbatim from ST I-II, q. 49, prol.

. . . felt his heart lighten from being closer to his friend.
For Aquinas, the virtue of charity was above all friendship-love for God
shared with others (see ST II-II, q. 23, a. 1). By all accounts, he was true
friends with Brother Reginald of Piperno (or Priverno). Aquinas dedi-
cated his *Compendium of Theology* to Reginald, his permanent *socius*, or
brother-companion, in the Order of Preachers, and called him "a very
dear son." Reginald was served as a "nurse" for Thomas, ensuring that he
would eat when necessary; he transcribed dictation at any time of day or
night; he walked with him on long journeys, such as from Paris to Rome;
and he even preached Thomas's funeral panegyric. See J. P. Torrell, *Saint
Thomas Aquinas: Person and His Work, Vol. 1*, rev. ed. (Washington, DC:
The Catholic University of America Press, 2005), 272–74. Reginald is
the chief link we have to Thomas's life: he spoke to all of his early biographers about him (Foster, *The Life of Saint Thomas Aquinas*, 3), and he
spoke to his mother about him—so much that Reginald's mother served
as a witness at the canonization inquiry (Torrell, *Saint Thomas Aquinas*,
26).

"The teaching of Thomas has become an object of admiration."
Foster, *The Life of Saint Thomas Aquinas*, 35.

Aquinas was phenomenally prolific.
Torrell, *Saint Thomas Aquinas*, 241.

"His memory was extremely rich and retentive."
Foster, *The Life of Saint Thomas Aquinas*, 51. Aquinas's memory serves
as an example for medieval mnemonic mastery in the rich and thoroughly engaging work of Mary Carruthers, *The Book of Memory: A Study
of Memory in Medieval Culture* (Cambridge, UK: Cambridge University
Press, 1990), especially in her introduction in which she compares the
genius of Einstein with that of Thomas.

. . . he was the "primary" human cause . . .
The theme of primary and secondary causality is prominent in Aquinas's
thought, including his explanations of God's providence in relation to
natural movement (e.g., ST I, q. 105, a. 4, ad 1 and a. 5), the operation
of grace in relation to free choice (e.g., ST I-II, q. 113, a. 3), and Christ's
soul in relation to his divinity (e.g., ST III, q. 7, a. 1, ad 3).

A habit is . . . the "intrinsic principle of human acts."
See ST I-II, prol.

. . . he was able to be who he was because of his habits.
As will be explained later on, some habits affect certain human powers—e.g., shaping our intellect or emotions—whereas others shape our
very being and so have been called "entiative" habits.

"A minimum of time allowed to sleeping and eating . . ."
Foster, *The Life of Saint Thomas Aquinas*, 37. This manifests the enormous power of Aquinas's habits and his total commitment to this way
of life.

No other great Catholic writer has a treatise on habits.
It's incredible but true. Probably because Aquinas was more committed
to developing a theory and explanation of human nature as a necessary
prerequisite to understanding morality, whereas nearly all others took
these issues for granted. In addition, Thomas developed the ethics of
Aristotle, the science of Galen, and of many other thinkers that were
often discounted by other scholars.

Another book on habits? There are so many out there.
My thinking on habits has been incalculably aided by many other writ-
ers, many of whom are listed in the bibliography of my longer work
Habits and Holiness: Ethics, Theology, and Biopsychology (Catholic Uni-
versity of America Press, 2020). Above all, Charles Duhigg's work *The
Power of Habit: Why We Do What We Do, and How to Change* (London:
Random House Books, 2013) was especially helpful, and I am indebted
to Nicholas Kahm for originally suggesting that I read the book. Whereas
Duhigg writes from the perspective of theory-poor behaviorist psychology, the other seminal book that affected my thinking on the topic is
Félix Ravaisson's short but incredibly insightful *Of Habit*, trans., intro,
and commentary by Clare Carlisle and Mark Sinclair (London: Con-
tinuum, 2008; org. 1838), which describes the pervasive and organic
nature of habit throughout all levels of life.

**Representing a scientific approach, William James in the nineteenth
century. . .**
Important works on habit from the perspective of empirical science
include William James's chapter on habit in *The Principles of Psychology*,

vol. 1 (New York: Henry Holt and Company, 1890), the essays collected in *The Psychology of Habit: Theory, Mechanisms, Change, and Contexts*, ed. Bas Verplanken (Springer, 2018), Ann M. Graybiel, "Habits, Rituals, and the Evaluative Brain," *Annual Review of Neuroscience* 31 (2008): 359–87, Wendy Wood and Dennis Rünger, "Psychology of Habit," *Annual Review of Psychology* 67 (2016): 289–314.

Then there are books that cover habit-theory in a deep and systematic way.
The best, by far, is Santiago Jacobus M. Ramirez, *Opera Omnia Tomus VI: De Habitibus in Communi: In I-II Summae Theologiae Divi Thomae Expositio* (QQ. 49-54), vols. I and II, ed. Victorino Rodriguez (Madrid: Instituto de Filosofia "Luis Vives", 1973). Very valuable also is George Klubertanz, *Habit and Virtue* (New York: Meredith Publishing Company, 1965).

As Aquinas states in his commentary on the book of Job . . .
Thomas Aquinas, *Expositio super Iob ad litteram* (Literal Exposition on Job), commentary on c. 1:7–9, my translation.

. . . the Angelic Doctor's work may indeed be hard and dry
Norman Kretzmann and Eleonore stump compare Aquinas's "hard and dry" work with a beetle shell in "Introduction," *The Cambridge Companion to Aquinas* (Cambridge, UK: Cambridge University Press, 1993), 6.

. . . my job would be to fish for one of those decapods . . .
Hunting, fishing, and tracking prey were typical tropes to describe memory recall: Carruthers, *The Book of Memory*, 247.

. . . *you* must be a Brother Reginald and your soul must be the vellum.
Writing and drawing were key mnemonic techniques for scholastics: Carruthers, *The Book of Memory*, 144, 241–42.

. . . for it will not only guide you to develop better atom-sized habits . . .
I draw upon the good work of James Clear, *Atomic Habits: An Easy and Proven Way to Build Good Habits and Break Bad Ones* (New York: Avery, 2018) but also provide much more than he does in terms of theory and practice.

God is an author as well.
This insight is partly inspired by a lesser-known portion of John Donne's famous Meditation XVII, "for whom the bell tolls," which reads, in part: "All mankind is of one author, and is one volume; when one man dies, one chapter is not torn out of the book, but translated into a better language; and every chapter must be so translated; God employs several translators; some pieces are translated by age, some by sickness, some by war, some by justice; but God's hand is in every translation, and his hand shall bind up all our scattered leaves again, for that library where every book shall lie open to one another."

. . . there were two authors of Scripture . . .
Faithful to Thomas's thought, these expressions are from Reginald Garrigou-Lagrange, *Reality: A Synthesis of Thomistic Thought*, trans. Patrick Cummins (St. Louis: B. Herder, 1950), 341–42.

". . . admirable instrument of the Holy Spirit."
Foster, *The Life of Saint Thomas Aquinas*, 131.

. . . algorithms to live by . . .
Whereas economics and programming worked to model and analyze human behavior through mathematical equations, now in a sort of a feedback loop, some argue that we should model our behavior on the models: Brian Christian and Tom Griffiths, *Algorithms to Live By: The Computer Science of Human Decisions* (London: William Collins, 2016). This exemplifies how rule-based thinking can reduce human life to robotic action.

Law has two primary purposes . . .
ST I-II, q. 90, a. 1, "Law is a rule and measure of acts, whereby man is induced to act or is restrained from acting."

Prudence is the habit of mental maturity . . .
Prudence is a virtue that requires thinking about one's actions and experience, hence maturity in thought; it separates men from boys: ST II-II, q. 47, a. 14, ad 3. Aquinas outlines mnemonic techniques while showing that good memory use is a part of prudence: ST II-II, q. 49, a. 1, ad 2.

. . . only two "rules of life" are absolutely necessary . . .
ST II-II, q. 44, a. 3.

... easily, quickly, sweetly, and skillfully ...
Acts performed with these qualities are signs of a well-developed habit:
ST I-II, q. 58, a. 1, ad 3; *De virtutibus* q. 1, a. 1, ad 13.

Chapter 2

A letter attributed to Aquinas ...
*How to Study: Being the Letter of St. Thomas Aquinas to Brother John
De Modo Studendi*, trans. Victor White (London: Aquin Press, 1960).
Although the letter is considered spurious in modern editions, neverthe-
less White points out that the principles are very much in harmony with
Aquinas's views on learning and the virtue of *studiositas*.

We walk in a world of symbols ...
See Emile Mâle, *The Gothic Image: Religious Art in Thirteenth Century
France* (New York: Harper, 1972), 14: "The third characteristic of medi-
aeval art lies in this, that it is a symbolic code. From the days of the
catacombs Christian art has spoken in figures, showing men one thing
and inviting them to see in it the figure of another. The artist, as the
doctors might have put it, must imitate God who under the letter of
Scripture hid profound meaning, and who willed that nature too should
hold lessons for man." Symbolic representations of the world exist in
every culture, but the symbolizing impulse is especially Christian, as
Christ reveals the Father as his perfect Image; and the Incarnation and
the sacraments are symbolic through and through.

**... a group of babies preferred triangles and circles that interacted
cooperatively ...**
The Yale study examined responses of six- and ten-month-old infants
to a scenario in which a triangle helped a circle up a hill and another
scenario in which a square tried to prevent a circle from ascending. They
consistently preferred the helping triangle to the hindering square. J.
Kiley Hamlin et al., "Social Evaluation by Preverbal Infants," *Nature*
450, no. 7169 (November 2007): 557–59. Infant evaluation of mod-
eled social morality was corroborated by another study: J. Kiley Hamlin
and Karen Wynn, "Young Infants Prefer Prosocial to Antisocial Others,"
Cognitive Development 26, no. 1 (2011): 30–39.

A model is a symbolic representation of a small set of ideas . . .

The definition is my own. See William A. Wallace, *The Modeling of Nature: Philosophy of Science and Philosophy of Nature in Synthesis* (Washington, DC: The Catholic University of America Press, 1996), xiii.

Models are enormously useful. They help us . . .

Scott E. Page, *The Model Thinker: What You Need to Know to Make Data Work for You* (New York: Basic Books, 2018), 6. Page uses the mnemonic REDCAPE, saying that models help us reason about objects of study, explain them, design new things, communicate knowledge and understanding, act with rational policies, predict future events, and explore possibilities.

. . . models that serve as analogies . . .

Models can also embody certain elements of an object (e.g., brain models) or function as "computational and analytic playgrounds" for exploration. Page, *The Model Thinker*, 13–14. For Aquinas, an analogy expresses a proportionality, comparison, or agreement between one thing and another, such that the referent possesses some reality that the referred possesses in its own way (see *De principiis naturae*, c. 6, n. 47). Mathematical models, Aquinas would say, abstract from the material and changeable reality of a thing and present its more formal aspects (see *Sententia Metaphysicae*, lib. 3, l. 7, n. 20 and l. 14).

My multi-model approach offers . . .

Page doesn't hide the fact that every model is imperfect because in its simplification of reality, it omits details that could be relevant to another analysis. However, the inaccuracy of a single model can be mitigated by utilizing multiple accurate models, which can provide a balance between overwhelming specificity and wandering generalities. *The Model Thinker*, 27–35. My approach goes a step beyond Page, for my many models fit with each other and build upon each other in an integrated manner, somewhat like the way Rudolf Carnap presents symbolic logic in successive stages in his classic work *Introduction to Symbolic Logic and Its Applications* (New York: Dover Publications, 1958).

E. L. Thorndike and B. F. Skinner

See Edward L. Thorndike, "Laws and Hypotheses of Behavior," in *Animal Intelligence: Experimental Studies* (New York: MacMillan, 1911), 241–81. B. F. Skinner, *The Behavior of Organisms: An Experimental*

Analysis (New York: Appleton-Century-Crofts, 1938); *Science and Human Behavior* (New York: Free Press, 1953); "What is the Experimental Analysis of Behavior?" *Journal of the Experimental Analysis of Behavior*, No. 9 (1966): 213–18.

To change or develop a habit, you can focus on one or all of the elements of a habit loop.
David L. Watson and Roland G. Tharp, *Self-Directed Behavior: Self-Modification for Personal Adjustment, 10th Edition* (Belmont, CA: Wadsworth, Cengage Learning: 2014), 14.

. . . we can act in *a fully human way* only by employing good habits.
See Aquinas, *De virtutibus in commune*, q. 1, a. 10, co; ST I-II, q. 49, a. 4.

St. Benedict . . . "pray always."
This example is mentioned in Giacomo Cardinal Lecaro, *Methods of Mental Prayer* (Westminster: Newman Press, 1957), 270.

. . . plans to avoid a habituated trigger-response typically do not lead to success.
See S. Orbell and V. Verplanken, "Progress and Prospects in Habit Research," in *The Psychology of Habit: Theory, Mechanisms, Change, and Contexts*, ed. Bas Verplanken (New York: Springer, 2018), 397–409 at 401.

. . . we are all philosophers. . .
Mortimer J. Adler, *How to Think about the Great Ideas*, ed. Max Weismann (Chicago and La Salle: Open Court, 2000), xiii.

"All men by nature desire to know."
Aristotle, *Metaphysics* I.1.

"Among all human pursuits, the pursuit of wisdom is . . . "
Summa Contra Gentiles [hereafter: SCG], I, c. 2, n. 1.

. . . there are two basic categories of human behavior . . . "human action" in contrast to "an action of a human."
ST I, q. 1, a. 1.

"As many arrows, loosed several ways. . . "
Henry V, act I, scene 2, lines 207–12.

St. Thomas Aquinas often uses the arrow as a model to explain action.
See, among many references, SCG III, c. 2, n. 2; ST I, q. 103, a. 1, ad 1 and ad 3; ST I-II, q. 1, a. 2; ST I-II, q. 12, a. 5; *De Veritate*, q. 5, a. 2.

Taken together, these three elements provide a linear model of human action . . .
The morality of the human act depends on its object, end, and circumstances. See ST I-II, q. 20, a. 3. See also the *Catechism of the Catholic Church*, nos. 1750–54. The chief element is the object: ST I-II, q. 18, a. 2; 19, a. 2.

. . . every action has its own piercing intelligibility or "object."
See *Veritatis Splendor: On Certain Fundamental Questions in the Moral Teaching of the Church* (1993), no. 78.

End: why you do it . . .
"Just as the target is the end for the archer, so is it the end for the motion of the arrow" (SCG, III, c. 2, n. 2).

Aquinas defines a habit . . .
See ST I-II, q. 49, a. 3.

. . . utilizing the habit loop can help people achieve their goals 66 percent to 84 percent of the time.
Watson and Tharp, *Self-Directed Behavior*, ix. It should be noted that this success rate regards behavioral goals, such as losing weight, studying more efficiently, exercising, and so on. The habit loop has been especially effective for Habit Reversal Therapy (HRT)—that is, eliminating the effects of undesired habits and replacing them with desired ones. See Douglas W. Woods and Raymond G. Miltenberger, "Habit Reversal: A Review of Applications and Variations," *Journal of Behavior Therapy and Experimental Psychiatry* 26, no. 2 (June 1, 1995): 123–31. Also, Karina S. Bate et al., "The Efficacy of Habit Reversal Therapy for Tics, Habit Disorders, and Stuttering: A Meta-Analytic Review," *Clinical Psychology Review* 31, no. 5 (July 2011): 865–71. It is unclear how successful the habit loop alone would be for more complex, interior goals such as

understanding Plato, management of PTSD, developing the virtue of prudence, or appreciating Debussy's piano works.

Efficient causes arrive first in time . . .
Commentary on Aristotle's Metaphysics, lib. 5, lect. 2, n. 13: "The efficient cause is related to the final cause because the efficient cause is the starting point of motion and the final cause is its terminus. . . . The final cause is the cause of the efficient cause, not in the sense that it makes it be, but inasmuch as it is the reason for the causality of the efficient cause. For an efficient cause is a cause inasmuch as it acts, and it acts only because of the final cause." For example, working (efficient cause) triggers Bobby to eat (final cause): if Bobby could not eat, then working would not be a trigger of eating; it would merely be a trigger of hunger or some other response. Hence, the real potential to eat is the reason why working can be a trigger of his actual eating.

. . . a thing is said to be perfect insofar as it attains its proper end.
ST II-II, q. 184, a. 1. Also, ST I-II, q. 1, a. 6.

. . . final cause, as the good toward which a person tends, impels a person to activate all the other causes to reach it.
See *Commentary on Aristotle's Metaphysics*, lib. 5, lect. 3, n. 6: "Although the end may be the final thing in some cases, it is always prior in causality. Hence it is called the 'cause of causes,' because it is the cause of the causality of all causes. For it is the cause of efficient causality . . . and the efficient cause is the cause of the causality of both the matter and the form."

. . . *fruition* is the pleasure a person experiences . . .
Daniel De Haan, "*Delectatio, gaudium, fruitio*: Three Kinds of Pleasure for Three Kinds of Knowledge in Thomas Aquinas," *Quaestio* 15 (2015): 543–52, at 544. See ST I-II, q. 11, a. 1.

Chapter 3

. . . slime molds . . .
See Andrew Adamatzky, "Slime mold solves maze in one pass, assisted by gradient of chemo-attractants," *IEEE Trans Nanobioscience*, No. 11(2) (2012):131–34. Tetsu Saigusa, et al., "Amoebae Anticipate Periodic

Events," *Physical Review Letters*, Vol. 100 (2008): 018101. David Vogel and Audrey Dussutour, "Direct transfer of learned behaviour via cell fusion in non-neural organisms," *Proc. R. Soc. B* 283: 20162382.

. . . a substantial and individual life-force which Aquinas recognized as an "animal soul."
See Aristotle, *De anima*, 415a1. See Aquinas, *Commentary on Aristotle's De Anima*, Book II, lectures 3 and 4.

Consider the jellyfish.
See Alex J. Yu and Catharine H. Rankin, "Nonassociative Learning in Invertebrates," in *The Oxford Handbook of Invertebrate Neurobiology*, ed. John H. Byrne (Oxford, UK: Oxford University Press, 2019), 513–36. Richard A. Satterlie, "Do Jellyfish Have Central Nervous Systems?" *The Journal of Experimental Biology* 214, no. Pt 8 (April 15, 2011): 1215–23. David J. Albert, "What's on the Mind of a Jellyfish? A Review of Behavioural Observations on Aurelia Sp. Jellyfish," *Neuroscience and Biobehavioral Reviews* 35, no. 3 (January 2011): 474–82.

As far back as 1885, George Romanes's research on jellyfish . . .
Juli Berwald, *Spineless: The Science of Jellyfish and the Art of Growing a Backbone* (New York: Riverhead Books, 2017), 138–40. See George J. Romanes, *Jelly-Fish, Star-Fish and Sea Urchins, Being a Research on Primitive Nervous Systems* (London: K. Paul, Trench & Co., 1885), 80–87. For more recent research, see Mary C. Johnson and Karl L. Wuensch, "An Investigation of Habituation in the Jellyfish Aurelia Aurita," *Behavioral and Neural Biology* 61, no. 1 (January 1, 1994): 54–59.

In 2000, Eric Kandel won the Nobel Prize . . .
See Eric R. Kandel, *Cellular Basis of Behavior: An Introduction to Behavioral Neurobiology* (San Francisco: W. H. Freeman and Co., 1976); "The Biology of Memory: A Forty-Year Perspective," *The Journal of Neuroscience* 29, no. 41 (October 14, 2009): 12748–56; "Biographical," *NobelPrize.org*, Nobel Media AB, https://www.nobelprize.org/prizes/medicine/2000/kandel/biographical.

You can teach an old dog trainer new tricks.
Cesar Millan, the TV personality and "dog whisperer" beloved in Hollywood, thanks his wife for teaching him to appreciate women more—thereby undoing habits he had gained in childhood. See Cesar Millan

and Melissa Jo Peltier, *Cesar's Way: The Natural, Everyday Guide to Understanding & Correcting Common Dog Problems* (New York: Three Rivers Press, 2006), 7. For studies on adult neurogenesis, see Fred H. Gage, "Structural Plasticity of the Adult Brain," *Dialogues in Clinical Neuroscience* 6, no. 2 (June 2004): 135–41. Yan Gu, Stephen Janoschka, and Shaoyu Ge, "Neurogenesis and Hippocampal Plasticity in Adult Brain," *Current Topics in Behavioral Neurosciences* 15 (2013): 31–48.

If a jellyfish develops dispositive habits to swim in a particular way, it still remains carefree, unlike us humans.
Here I am reminded of G. K. Chesterton's poem entitled "Troilet" in *The Coloured Lands: Fairy Stories, Comic Verse and Fantastic Pictures* (Mineola, NY: Dover Publications, 2009; original: 1938). 92.

"Man does many things without deliberation . . ."
ST I-II, q. 1, a. 1, obj. 3. Also, SCG III, c. 2, n. 9.

". . . the world's loneliest elephant . . ."
"'World's Loneliest Elephant' Gets Green Light to Seek New Life - and Companionship," *Sky News*, 6 September 2020, https://news.sky.com/story/worlds-loneliest-elephant-gets-green-light-to-seek-new-life-and-companionship-12064856. Alia Chughtai, "Pakistan to Free Elephant Kaavan after Campaign by US Singer Cher," *Al Jazeera*, 22 May 2020, https://www.aljazeera.com/news/2020/05/pakistan-free-elephant-kaavan-campaign-singer-cher-200522082957974.html. Although she was nearly aborted by her mother, Cher admits to aborting one of her children, and she advocates for Planned Parenthood. Nancy Mills, "Wild Child Cher & Her Child Singer Talks of Family Life," *New York Daily News*, 22 September 1996, https://www.nydailynews.com/wild-child-cher-child-singer-talks-family-life-eve-hbo-controversial-abortion-movie-article-1.738756. Her daughter, Chastity Bono, underwent female-to-male gender surgery, and now identifies as a man named Chaz.

In our time, more and more people recognize with Aquinas that some animals are "higher" than others . . .
In Aquinas's view, a "nobler" soul is what constitutes a higher animal; the quality of soul is manifested in the animal's behavior. See *Commentary on Aristotle's* De Anima, Book 2, lect. 6, n. 2. According to Aquinas, it is the nobler soul that calls for more complex, "more distinctly diversified, organs or bodily instruments." *Commentary on Aristotle's* De Anima,

Book 1, lect. 14, no. 10. For Carl Safina, the physiological structure that enables complex behavior constitutes an adequate criterion of a higher order of animal. His language implies that all vertebrates are "higher": "Animals with backbones (fishes, amphibians, reptiles, birds, and mammals) all share the same basic skeleton, organs, nervous systems, hormones, and behaviors. Just as different models of automobiles each have an engine, drive train, four wheels, doors, and seats, we differ mainly in terms of our outside contours and a few internal tweaks. But like naïve car buyers, most people see only animals' varied exteriors." *Beyond Words: What Animals Think and Feel* (London: Souvenir Press, 2020), 20.

Elephants . . . manifest panic . . .
See Safina, *Beyond Words*, 11–107.

An emotion is "about" something.
Heather Lench and Zari Carpenter, "What Do Emotions Do for Us?" in *The Function of Emotions: When and Why Emotions Help Us*, ed. Heather C. Lench, (New York, NY: Springer, 2018), 1–7 at 3.

Chemical correlates of emotions . . .
See Loretta Graziano Breuning's popular work *Habits of a Happy Brain: Retrain Your Brain to Boost Your Serotonin, Dopamine, Oxytocin, & Endorphin Levels* (Avon, Massachusetts: Adams Media, 2015). Although a useful introduction to how brain, emotions, and chemicals interact, this work erroneously it equates emotions with the chemicals correlative to them.

Randolph Nesse notes . . .
Randolph M. Ness, *Good Reasons for Bad Feelings: Insights from the Frontier of Evolutionary Psychiatry* (London: Penguin, 2020), 54. Ibid., the other Nesse quotation in the same paragraph.

. . . emotions are distinguished by the sorts of objects to which they respond.
ST I-II, q. 41, a. 2. See ST I-II, q. 22, a. 2, co. and ad 3.

Good is ultimately attractive, and bad is repulsive. The most basic emotion is some sort of love for the good.
ST I-II, q. 23, a. 4. For the taxonomy of emotions, see ST I-II, q. 23, a. 1.

Even less intelligent animals such as chickens . . .
Recent studies have shown that chickens have a more complex emotional, social, and cognitive life than previously realized. They even demonstrate having different individual temperaments. Lori Marino, "Thinking Chickens: A Review of Cognition, Emotion, and Behavior in the Domestic Chicken," *Animal Cognition* 20, no. 2 (2017): 127–47. Laura Garnham and Hanne Løvlie, "Sophisticated Fowl: The Complex Behaviour and Cognitive Skills of Chickens and Red Junglefowl," *Behavioral Sciences* 8, no. 1 (January 17, 2018), 13, https://doi.org/10.3390/bs8010013.

. . . emotions "have their own proper movements" and practically "have a will of their own" . . . ST I-II, q. 56, a. 4, ad 3.

. . . the animal's estimation, emotions, and behavior participate in the rational agency of the trainer.
ST I-II, q. 50, a. 3, ad 2, and q. 1, a. 2.

Nature literature is fraught with anthropomorphism . . .
Carl Safina discusses the issue at length in *Beyond Words*, 26–30. Later in the book, though, he commits the same fault or approvingly quotes others who do. The example is from ibid., 47. There are many other examples throughout the text.

"animals are people too"
Animals Are People Too: An Adorable Animal Emotion Thesaurus (New York: Odd Dot, 2019). Dave Aftandilian, "Animals Are People, Too: Ethical Lessons about Animals from Native American Sacred Stories," Interdisciplinary Humanities, Vol. 27, Issue 1 (2010): 79–98.

Humans are animals too: *rational* animals.
ST I, q. 29, a. 1, ad 2: "The term that refers sometimes to the nature expressed by the definition, as when we ask, *What is man?* and we answer: *A mortal rational animal.*" Also: "the notions of animal and man do not differ in animality but rather in man's rational principle that he has over and above animality." *Commentary on Aristotle's Nicomachean Ethics*, Book I, lect. 7, n. 2.

We share some traits and powers in common with beasts, especially estimation and emotion.

In order help readers grasp its basic functioning, I use the name "estimative power" for that which exists in both humans and animals. The estimative power helps an animal judge a situation as beneficial or harmful, as well as other percepts that urge it toward actions such as fight, flight, freezing, or befriending. In humans, Aquinas calls it the "cogitative power," giving it a different name to indicate that as a part of the human system, and rooted in the rational soul, it has more functions and a fundamentally different orientation than that which exists in sub-rational beings. See ST I, q. 78, a. 4, co. and ad 5.

Aquinas explains the difference between beast-knowledge and human-knowledge . . .
ST II-II, q. 8, a. 1.

British analytic philosopher P. M. S. Hacker . . .
The first quotes are from P. M. S. Hacker, *Human Nature: The Categorial Framework* (Oxford: Wiley-Blackwell, 2010), 202 and 203. The second quote is from *The Intellectual Powers: A Study of Human Nature* (Oxford: Wiley-Blackwell, 2013), 395.

Our concepts transcend particular and perceptible objects . . .
See Mortimer J. Adler, *The Difference of Man and the Difference It Makes* (New York: Fordham University Press, 1993), 157.

Aquinas calls it the "rational appetite."
See ST I, q. 80, a. 2; I-II, q. 1, a. 2; q. 8, a. 1, and many other places.

A being that can act for reasons is *responsible* for its actions.
P. M. S. Hacker, *The Intellectual Powers*, 394.

The fourth-century Catholic bishop . . .
Nemesius, *On the Nature of Man*, trans. R. W. Sharples and P. J. van der Eijk (Liverpool: Liverpool University Press, 2008), 175.

. . .habits are *necessary* for our full perfection . . .
ST I-II, q. 49, a. 4.

Aquinas notes that our habits take us either downward or upward.
Commentary on Aristotle's Ethics, Book 7, lect. 1, n. 5.

While awaiting execution in 1535, More penned a long work . . .
Thomas More, *A Dialogue of Comfort against Tribulation*, revised by
Mary Gottschalk (Strongsville, OH: Scepter, 1998), 271–72.

**More's explanation of the beneficial work of good habits came from
his own experience.**
The following quotations are taken from E. E. Reynolds, *Saint Thomas
More* (New York: Image Books, 1958), 251–54 passim.

Plato . . . the first Western thinker to discuss the soul . . .
Aristotle is typically considered the first psychologist properly speaking
because he wrote an entire treatise devoted to the soul, *De anima*. Pla-
tonists, however, argue that Plato's *Republic* is as much about the soul
as it is politics. I won't here try to adjudicate this fight over honorifics.
My exposition comes from *Republic* IX, 588b-e. Plato uses other images
to explain the soul, including the famous image of the charioteer who
drives two horses: *Phaedrus* 246a-248b.

**Just as the lion was considered by the ancients as strong and noble
. . .**
See, for example, ST I, q. 13, aa. 6 and 9; I-II, q. 46, a. 5, ad 1. Also,
Commentary on Isaiah, ch. 11, lect. 2, n. 369.

**Aquinas states, "For the sensitive appetite is naturally moved not
only . . . in man by the cogitative [estimative] power . . ."**
ST I, q. 81, a. 3, ad 2.

**Gregory the Great argues that "the movements of the flesh" are like
beasts . . .**
Moralia in Iob (Moral Commentary on the Book of Job), Book VI, c.
33, n. 51.

**St. Thomas explains, "The inclination to sin is a punishment for sin
. . ."**
Commentary on Romans, ch. 7, lect. 4, n. 587. The word for "inclination"
here in Latin is *fomes*, which literally is "kindling for a fire"; the idea is
that this inclination or readiness to sin can be "lit up" by one's deliberate
choice.

He also notes that just as "fierceness" can be considered a sort of law for dogs . . .
ST I-II, q. 91, a. 6.

When we are united with a desired good and feel pleasure . . . we are also more attached to that good.
See Aquinas, *Commentary on Aristotle's Nicomachean Ethics*, Book 2, lect. 3, n. 1. Also, *De veritate*, q. 20, a. 2.

Studies suggest that when a person is habituated . . . the neurotransmitter chemicals . . .
Breuning, *Habits of a Happy Brain*, 34. The mere presence of oxytocin and dopamine in the brain do not constitute a reward on their own: the decisive factor is how the chemicals affect neurons that *have already* been wired for approach or avoidance. See Ralph Adolphs and David J. Anderson, *The Neuroscience of Emotion: A New Synthesis* (Princeton, NJ: Princeton University Press, 2018), 200.

Lost people, trained to theoretic feud!
William Wordsworth, "The Warning," lines 111–12, 119–20 in *The Poems of William Wordsworth: Collected Readings from the Cornell Wordsworth*, Vol. 3, ed. Jared Curtis (Ithaca, NY: Cornell University Press), 700.

Perhaps this is why it has been said that we should distrust all in whom the impulse to punish is powerful.
Friedrich Nietzsche, *Thus Spoke Zarathustra* in *The Portable Nietzsche*, ed. and trans. Walter Kaufmann (New York: Viking Penguin, 1982), 212.

Such was the view of the quintessential Stoics . . .
For the following exposition, see Richard Sorabji, *Emotion and Peace of Mind: From Stoic Agitation to Christian Temptation* (Oxford, UK: Oxford University Press), esp. 181–86.

"Stability," says the Controller . . .
Aldous Huxley, *Brave New World, Brave New World Revisited* (New York: Harper & Row, 1960), 31–32, 184.

Temple Grandin . . . illustrates the problems with anthropomorphism vividly.
Temple Grandin and Catherine Johnson, *Animals in Translation: The Woman Who Thinks Like a Cow* (London: Bloomsbury, 2005), 15.

"Whoever fights monsters . . ."
Friedrich Nietzsche, *Beyond Good and Evil* in *The Basic Writings of Nietzsche,* ed. and trans. Walter Kaufmann (New York: The Modern Library, 1992), no. 146.

The medieval friar summarizes: The Philosopher says . . .
(*Politics* I, c. 2) ST I-II, q. 17, a. 7. See *Republic* II, 358c.

Applying this political lesson to habituation . . .
See Aquinas, *Commentary on Aristotle's Politics*, Book I, lect. 1, n. 5.

Chapter 4

A serpent wrapped itself seven times around the body of Siddhārtha Gautama, called the Buddha.
Story and quotes in this paragraph from *The Life of the Buddha: According to the Pali Canon*, trans. and ed. Bhikku Ñānamoli (Onalaska, WA: BPS Pariyatti Editions 1992), 33–34.

It is not uncommon to read in newspapers or magazines . . .
Basis of these claims includes the following studies: Judson A. Brewer et al., "Meditation Experience Is Associated with Differences in Default Mode Network Activity and Connectivity," *Proceedings of the National Academy of Sciences* 108, no. 50 (December 13, 2011): 20254–59. Madhav Goyal et al., "Meditation Programs for Psychological Stress and Well-Being: A Systematic Review and Meta-Analysis," *JAMA Internal Medicine* 174, no. 3 (March 1, 2014): 357–68. So-An Lao, David Kissane, and Graham Meadows, "Cognitive Effects of MBSR/MBCT: A Systematic Review of Neuropsychological Outcomes," *Consciousness and Cognition* 45 (October 1, 2016): 109–23.

. . . the fundamental practice of mindfulness, as explained by the Buddha . . .

Walpola Sri Rahula, *What the Buddha Taught*, rev. ed. (New York: Grove Press, 1974), quoting "The Foundations of Mindfulness" (*Satipattha-na-sutta*), 109–19, and "Getting Rid of All Cares and Troubles (*Sab-basaa-sutta*), 101.

Perhaps this is why studies show that, in addition to positive outcomes of mindfulness . . .

More recent studies have noted that many studies of mindfulness lack scientific rigor and that a more careful evaluation shows negative effects of the practice as well. See Jared R. Lindahl et al., "The Varieties of Contemplative Experience: A Mixed-Methods Study of Meditation-Related Challenges in Western Buddhists," *PLOS ONE* 12, no. 5 (May 24, 2017): e0176239. Nicholas T. Van Dam et al., "Mind the Hype: A Critical Evaluation and Prescriptive Agenda for Research on Mindfulness and Meditation," *Perspectives on Psychological Science* Vol. 13, Issue 1 (2018): 36-61. M. Farias et al., "Adverse Events in Meditation Practices and Meditation-Based Therapies: A Systematic Review," *Acta Psychiatrica Scandinavica* (2020):1–19, https://doi.org/10.1111/acps.13225.

"every living thing gives proof of its life by that operation which is most proper to it . . ."

ST II-II, q. 179, a. 1.

"Christ also instructs within . . ."

Commentary on John, ch. 3, lect. 1, no. 428.

As St. Bonaventure beautifully said . . .

See his sermon V, *Christus unus omnium magister* in *Opera Theologica Selecta*, Vol. 5 (Florence, IT: Quaracchi, 1964), 295–307. Among other biblical verses, he refers to the Vulgate version of *Ecclesiasticus* 1:5, in Douay-Rheims translation: "The word of God on high is the fountain of wisdom." Also, 1 Cor 1:24, 30: "Christ the power of God and the wisdom of God. . . . He is the source of your life in Christ Jesus, whom God made our wisdom, our righteousness and sanctification and redemption." Mt 23:10: "You have one master, the Christ." Heb 1:3: "[The Son of God] is the refulgence of his glory, the very imprint of his being, and who sustains all things by his mighty word."

The Stoics held that to calm one's feelings . . .
This was apparently the position of Chrysippus and Cicero, though Seneca held a more nuanced view. See Sorabji, *Emotion and Peace of Mind*, 17–65 and 211–20.

Cognitive Therapy is similar.
Since its founding by Aaron Beck in the 1960s, cognitive therapy has become united with behaviorist techniques and now is typically referred to as cognitive behavioral therapy. David J. A. Dozios and Jay K. Brinker, "Cognitive Therapies," in *The Encyclopedia of Clinical Psychology*, ed. Robin L. Cautin and Scott O. Lilienfeld (Oxford: Wiley Blackwell, 2015), 656–65 at 656.

. . . it is not always easy for people to make proper distinctions.
The following examples are adapted from Richard L. Leahy, *Cognitive Therapy Techniques: A Practitioner's Guide*, Second Edition (New York: The Guilford Press, 2017), 21.

. . . there is a distinction between what Aquinas calls "extrinsic" versus "intrinsic" principles of human action.
ST I-II, q. 6, a. 1, ad 1 and 2.

. . . for by our thought we can moderate or even instigate our anger, fear, and other emotions. ST I, q. 81, a. 3.

Here, the A-B-C pattern of the habit loop may prove useful.
I adapt the chart in Leahy, *Cognitive Therapy Techniques*, 22. For a similar perspective, see Albert Ellis, Daniel David, and Steven Jay Lynn, "Rational and Irrational Beliefs: A Historical and Conceptual Perspective," in *Rational and Irrational Beliefs: Research, Theory, and Clinical Practice*, ed. Daniel David et al. (Oxford, UK: Oxford University Press, 2010), 3–22.

Aquinas defines a true statement as . . .
See ST I, q. 16, a. 2; a. 8, ad 3.

. . . man is a being of development: one must learn how to fulfill one's end . . .
Newman, *An Essay in Aid of A Grammar of Assent* (Notre Dame, IN: Notre Dame Press, 1979; org. 1870), 189.

... a "law of progress" as well as a "gift" and a "sacred duty" ...
A Grammar of Assent, 274.

Human reason naturally asks why things are the way they are ...
John Paul II, *Fides et Ratio*, 3.

"the soul ... reaches to the understanding of truth by arguing"
ST I, q. 79, a. 4. He also states, "The knowledge proper to the human soul is through the way of reasoning"—that is, the "investigation of reason," which separates from God who does not reason but knows things immediately and completely: *De Veritate*, q. 15, a. 1.

... we *understand*; that is, we apprehend intelligible truth, especially the essence of a thing.
ST I, q. 79 a. 8. Also, Aquinas, *Commentary on Aristotle's On Interpretation*, prologue.

"to reason is to advance from one thing understood to another ..."
ST I, q. 79 a. 8. Aquinas states the in same place that the very fact that we are able to string together such arguments in order to reach an abstract insight is why we are called "rational animals": "Man arrives at the knowledge of intelligible truth by advancing from one thing to another. Thus, he is called rational."

According to Newman, our most natural mode of reasoning ...
A Grammar of Assent, 260.

This natural mode of reasoning is therefore very personal: "an intellectual question ..."
Newman, *A Grammar of Assent*, 240.

Logic produces many useful outcomes ...
Newman, *A Grammar of Assent*, 228.

There are, therefore, significant advantages to logical reasoning.
A Grammar of Assent, 210–11.

... a demonstration is "a syllogism making one to know."
Summa Contra Gentiles I, c. 57, no. 5.

. . . one that takes the form commonly called *modus tollens* . . .
See William T. Parry and Edward A. Hacker, *Aristotelian Logic* (Albany: State University of New York Press, 1991), 374–76.

As Newman observes, when there is a difficulty in pursuing the truth . . .
A Grammar of Assent, 217.

When directing a stage production, Jack Marshall says . . .
See his blog post, "When The Truth Hurts, But A Lie Will Hurt More," *ethicsalarms.com*, 14 March 2014, https://ethicsalarms.com/2014/03/14/when-the-truth-hurts-but-a-lie-will-hurt-more.

John Paul II explained, "People cannot be genuinely indifferent . . ."
Fides et Ratio, 25.

St. Augustine shrewdly observed . . .
Confessions, Bk. X, c. 23, n. 33.

"intellectual virtues"
See ST I-II, q. 57; *Commentary on Aristotle's Nicomachean Ethics*, Book VI, esp. lectures 3–6.

. . . *opinion* is a mere conjecture we hold about something . . .
See ST I, q. 79, a. 9, ad 4.

The higher principles are more general . . .
See ST I, q. 79, aa. 9, 11.

Whereas a *maxim* is an abstract principle . . .
For an explanation of maxims and endoxa, see Eddo Rigotti and Sara Greco, *Inference in Argumentation: A Topics-Based Approach to Argument Schemes* (New York, NY: Springer, 2018), 214–18. They develop ideas found in Aristotle, *Topics*, Book I, c. 1, 100b21.

The mind needs some principle to organize the myriad impressions it receives . . .
"Bearing of Other Branches of Knowledge on Theology," in *The Idea of a University* (London: Longmans, Green, and Co., 1907), 75–76.

Newman argues that "though it is no easy matter to view things correctly . . ."
Ibid., 57. For his brief discussion of "stand-point," see *A Grammar of Assent*, 249.

. . . *weltanschauung* (worldview) as explained by Heidegger . . .
Quoted in Pascal David, "Weltanschauung," in *Dictionary of Untranslatables: A Philosophical Lexicon*, ed. Barbara Cassin, trans. Emily Apter et al. (Princeton, NJ: Princeton University Press, 2014), 1224–25.

As explained by Jeffrey E. Young and his colleagues, a schema . . .
Jeffrey E. Young, Janet S. Klosko, and Marjorie E. Weishaar, *Schema Therapy: A Practitioner's Guide* (New York; London: The Guilford Press, 2006), 6. I provide a synthesis of the various descriptions/definitions of "schema" provided by the authors. Their comprehensive notion of a schema is preferable to that of Aaron Beck, which seems to reduce everything to a cognitive reality. See *Cognitive Therapy of Personality Disorders*, Third Edition, ed. Aaron T. Beck, Denise D. Davis, Arthur Freeman (New York: The Guilford Press, 2015), 33–41.

. . . for persons "regard schemas as *a priori* truths . . ."
Young, et al., *Schema Therapy*, 8.

The dystopian and prescient novel George Orwell, *Nineteen Eighty-Four* . . .
(New York: Signet, 1983; org. 1949), 198–200.

The Party called this deeply ingrained habit *crimestop*.
Orwell, *Nineteen Eighty-Four*, 229.

As Ellis notes, once generated, the consequences of one habit loop . . .
Ellis et al., "Rational and Irrational Beliefs: A Historical and Conceptual Perspective," 4.

On the night of 8 October 1845 . . .
This account is substantially that of Cardinal Alfonso Capecelatro, an Oratorian contemporary of the two men, as quoted in Aldo Lippi, "A Providential Encounter: Newman and the Passionists," *Passionist International Bulletin*, N° 23 (June-Settembre

2010):   7–12,   http://www.newmanfriendsinternational.org/
en/26th-august-feast-of-blessed-dominic-barberi/.

Father Barberi later wrote . . .
Quoted in Kevin O'Brien, "Reflections on Newman and the Intellectual Tradition," in *Newman and the Intellectual Tradition: The Portsmouth
Review 2010*, ed. James P. MacGuire (Lanham: Sheed & Ward: 2013),
116–19 at 118.

As a young Anglican clergyman, Newman boldly declared . . .
Quoted in David Newsome, *The Convert Cardinals: John Henry
Newman and Henry Edward Manning* (London: John Murray,
1993), 134.

In 1840, five years before his conversion, Newman had written . . .
"The Catholicity of the Anglican Church," *British Critic* (1840), later
included in his *Essays Critical and Historical*, Vol. 2 (London: Longmans,
Green, and Co., 1907), 1–73 at 71.

Charles Kingsley would challenge Newman's sincerity . . .
The subject of Kingsley's attack was ostensibly Newman's writings on
how Catholics treat the truth, but Newman's adoption of the Catholic faith upon his conversion was central to Kingsley's claims. Kingsley
writes, "There is a great deal to be said for that view," that Newman is
entirely untrustworthy, "now that Dr. Newman has become (one must
needs suppose) suddenly, and since the 1st of February, 1864, a convert
to the economic views [of truth] of St. Alfonso da Liguori and his com-
peers. I am henceforth in doubt and fear, as much as an honest man can
be, concerning every word Dr. Newman may write." Kingsley, "What,
Then, Does Dr. Newman Mean?" in John Henry Newman, *Apologia Pro
Vita Sua: A Norton Critical Edition*, ed. David J. DeLaura (New York:
W. W. Norton & Company, 1968), 310–40 at 337. All quotations from
Newman's *Apologia* are from this edition.

**That text quotes a letter he had written nearly a year before his con-
version . . .**
Letter of 16 November 1844, in *Apologia Pro Vita Sua*, 177.

**"It should be considered whether such change is not *necessary*, if
truth be a real objective thing . . ."**

Letter of 3 April 1844, quoted in *Apologia Pro Vita Sua*, 161.

He became Catholic not to avoid some terrible punishment . . .
Preface to *Apologia Pro Vita Sua*, 7.

**"all true conversion must begin with the first springs of thought. . . .
Your whole nature must be re-born . . ."**
Apologia Pro Vita Sua, 191.

"strict obedience to the light"
Newman, *Arians of the Fourth Century* (London: Longmans, Green, and Co., 1908), 137.

Newman saw that a Catholic, layman or priest, is not indifferent to the Church's teaching . . . See *Apologia Pro Vita Sua*, 197.

"It is the very law of the human mind," he said, "in its inquiry after and acquisition of truth . . ."
Newman, "Christianity and Scientific Investigation," in *The Idea of a University*, 474.

"is a great and firm belief in the sovereignty of Truth . . ."
The Idea of a University, 478.

His conversion, he said, "was like coming into port after a rough sea."
This and the following quotation from *Apologia Pro Vita Sua*, 184.

A more thorough examination of mental habits would include an account of the intellectual virtues given by St. Thomas
See especially ST I-II, q. 57; *Commentary on Aristotle's Nicomachean Ethics*, Book VI, esp. lectures 3–6.

Ultimately, we shall find, as Cornelius à Lapide said, "The thought of wisdom . . ."
Cornelius à Lapide, *Commentaria in Scripturam Sacram, Tomus Octavus: In Canticum Canticorum et Librum Sapientiae* (Paris: Ludovicus Vivès, 1860), 407.

Chapter 5

According to another writer, heroes had a "liminal nature" . . .
Plutarch, "La Decadenza degli Oracoli," in *Tutti i Moralia*, ed. Emanuele Lelli and Giuliano Pisani (Milan: Bompiani, 2017), 416C. My translation.

Heroes were not worshipped as gods . . .
See Emily Kearns, "hero-cult" in *The Oxford Classical Dictionary*, Third Edition, eds. Simon Hornblower and Antony Spawforth (Oxford, UK: Oxford University Press, 1999), 693–94.

Aristotle, following Hesiod and Homer, describes a hero . . .
Nicomachean Ethics VII.1, 1145a28. Ibid., 1145a19.

Herodotus emphasizes . . .
The Landmark Herodotus: The Histories, ed. Robert Bl. Strassler, trans. Andrea L. Purvis (New York: Anchor Books, 2005), 7.139.6. Translation slightly modified for clarity. The other quotations in this paragraph are from 7.226.1 and 7.210.2 respectively.

The adage of Lord Acton . . .
Lord John Dalberg-Acton, *Letter to Archbishop Mandell Creighton*, 5 April 1887, http://oll.libertyfund.org/titles/acton-acton-creighton-correspondence.

Alexander the Great seems to exemplify Acton's adage . . .
The following description is from *The Landmark Arrian: The Campaigns of Alexander*, ed. James Romm, trans. Pamela Mensch (New York: Anchor Books, 2010).

He certainly was "a man . . ."
The Landmark Arrian, 7.30.1.

Thomas Aquinas explains that power . . .
De Potentia, q. 1, a. 1, co.

The higher a being is, the more it has power . . .
Ptolemy of Lucca, *On the Government of Rulers: De Regimine Principum*, trans. James M. Blythe (Philadelphia: University of Pennsylvania Press, 1997), III.1.4, p. 147.

Because God's being is perfect, there is no potential within him . . .
See *De Potentia*, q. 1, a. 7, co.

He is the cause and source of all power . . .
Pseudo-Dionysius, *The Divine Names* in *The Complete Works*, trans. Colm Luibheid and Paul Rorem (Mahwah, NY: Paulist Press, 1987),8.1-2.

All goods can be divided into three categories . . .
See Aristotle, *Politics* VII.1.

All of this created power comes ultimately from God's power: "In short . . ."
Pseudo-Dionysius, *The Divine Names*, 8.5.

. . . limited external goods: "where there is too much of them . . ."
Aristotle, *Politics* VII.1, 1323b7-11.

Evil, *qua* evil, never produces being or birth.
Pseudo-Dionysius, *The Divine Names*, 4.20.

. . . *megalopsychia*, literally, greatness of soul . . .
See the discussion in *Nicomachean Ethics* IV.3-4. The term is inaccurately translated as "pride" in the Revised Oxford Translation, edited by Jonathan Barnes (Princeton, NJ: Princeton University Press, 1984), but accurately translated in Aristotle, *Nicomachean Ethics*, trans. and ed. Sarah Broadie and Christopher Rowe (Oxford, UK: Oxford University Press, 2002).

Greatness of soul is "a sort of crown . . ."
Nicomachean Ethics IV.3, 1124a3-4.

One can define a heroic habit as, "a disposition . . ."
Howard J. Curzer, *Aristotle and the Virtues* (Oxford, UK: Oxford University Press, 2012), 142.

Philosopher Howard Curzer argues . . .
Curzer, *Aristotle and the Virtues*, 142.

Curzer's interpretation fits remarkably well with the Catholic understanding of virtue . . .
See the comment of Cardinal Capisucchi, "We must premise that heroic virtue is that which, either because of the excellence of the work, or the presence of some circumstance which makes the work very difficult, exhibits itself in some act which surpasses the ordinary human standard of working, so that a man is said to work heroically when he works beyond the ordinary measure even of men working virtuously." Quoted in Prospero Lambertini/Benedict XIV, *Heroic Virtue: A Portion of the Treatise on the Beatification and Canonization of the Servants of God*, trans. anonymous (London: Thomas Richardson and Son, 1850), 22–23.

As Thomas says, the greatest . . .
See ST II-II, q. 129, a 1, ad 3.

A truly great-souled person performs his great acts with humility . . .
See ST II-II, q. 129, a. 3, ad 4.

Christ is the "primordial exemplar" . . .
Aquinas, *Commentary on I Corinthians*, c. 11, l. 1, n. 583.

On account of the imperfection of the current state of the world, "the clarity of the saints . . ." Aquinas, *Commentary on Job*, c. 20, l. 2, v. 29.

St. Anthony Mary Claret . . .
Anthony Mary Claret y Clara, *Autobiography*, trans. and ed. José Maria Viñas (Chicago, Ill: Claretian Publications, 1976), nos. 226–27.

Although any person close to God possesses the good habits of virtue . . .
Lambertini, *Heroic Virtue*, 2. The following two quotations are from this work, 19, 20, and 24, respectively. Translation slightly changed for clarity.

In a similar way, without grace, a person's soul cannot be healed . . .
Disputed Questions on Truth, q. 28, a. 2.

Following St. Augustine, St. Thomas recalls Christ's healing . . .
Commentary on John, c. 9, l. 1, n. 1311.

St. Gertrude of Helfta . . .
The following is an adaptation of her account in *The Life and Revelations of Saint Gertrude*, trans. Poor Clares of Kenmare (London: Burns, Oates, and Washbourne, 1865), 71–74.

Whereas grace is a general supernatural habit . . .
ST II-II, q. 4, a. 1.

Faith gives the mind a certitude and firmness . . .
See Aquinas, *Commentary on Hebrews*, c. 11, l. 1, n. 558.

. . . faith provides us with the principles for overcoming temptation . . .
See *Exposition on the Apostles' Creed*, prol.: "The first thing that is necessary for every Christian is faith, without which no one is truly called a faithful Christian. Faith brings about four good effects. . . ."

Thomas explains that this command regards the perfection *necessary for salvation* . . .
See *On the Perfection of the Spiritual Life*, c. 5.

Charity involves a choice of the will informed by faith . . .
SCG IV, c. 54, n. 6.

. . . but human and divine love are naturally ordered.
ST II-II, q. 26.

. . . the command to love our neighbor is "like" the command to love God . . .
ST II-II, q. 44, a. 7.

"It can be argued that, if any man does not love his neighbor . . ."
ST II-II, q. 26, a. 2, ad 1.

Augustine expressed the balanced and correct view . . .
See his *Sermon* 169, n. 11 (13) (PL: 38:923), "Qui ergo fecit te sine te, non te iustificat sine te."

Michael Sherwin identifies five traits . . .
Such habits include skills and virtues. See Michael Sherwin, "Virtue as Creative Freedom and Emotional Wisdom," *Edification* 6, no. 1 (2012): 32–35, at 32–33.

"preserved cognitive control of expert performance"
K. Anders Ericsson, "Development of Elite Performance and Deliberate Practice: An Update from the Perspective of the Expert Performance Approach," in *Expert Performance in Sports: Advances in Research on Sport Expertise*, ed. Janet L. Starkes and K. Anders Ericsson (Champaign, IL: Human Kinetics, 2003), 49–84 at 61. The remainder of the paragraph relies on this article.

He is considered to be . . . in the words of Pope Benedict XVI . . .
Quoting Prosper of Aquitaine in his *General Audience on Saint Jerome (2)*, 14 November 2007, http://www.vatican.va/holy_father/benedict_xvi/audiences/2007/documents/hf_ben-xvi_aud_20071114_en.html.

. . . it has been noted that "Jerome took considerable pride . . ."
Michael Graves, *Jerome's Hebrew Philology: A Study Based on His Commentary on Jeremiah* (Leiden, Boston: Brill, 2007), 13. See *Letter* 84, n. 3; 50, nn. 1–2.

When I was a young man . . .
Letter 125, no. 12, in *Select Letters of St. Jerome*, trans. F. A. Wright (London: William Heineman; New York: G. P. Putnam's Sons, 1933), 419–21.

In a different letter . . .
Letter 22, no. 30, in *Select Letters of St. Jerome*, 129.

In his mind no certainty . . .
Quoted in Lambertini, *Heroic Virtue*, 84.

Lambertini notes that heroic charity . . .
Lambertini, *Heroic Virtue*, 114, 112.

St. Zélie, wrote: "Even Thérèse . . ."
This was written 9 June 1895. *Story of A Soul*, trans. John Clarke (Washington DC: ICS Publications, 1976), 276.

Following ancient tradition, Aquinas describes the growth of charity . . .
See ST II-II, q. 24, a. 9.

Those who have been transformed by charity desire "to be dissolved . . ."
ST II-II, q. 24, a. 9. This phrase is taken from the Vulgate version of Phil 1:23–24.

It is important to insist that the love of God spills over into the love of neighbor . . .
The three ways are enumerated in ST II-II, q. 44, a. 7.

Aquinas beautifully explains . . .
ST II-II, q. 23, a. 1, ad 2.

"a man should not give way to his neighbor in evil, but only . . ."
ST II-II, q. 44, a. 7.

Alexander the Great visited the philosopher Diogenes of Sinope . . .
See *The Landmark Arrian* 7.2.1-2. Also, Plutarch, *Lives*, vol. 2, trans. John Dryden, ed. Arthur Hugh Clough (New York: Modern Library, 2001), 149.

All must climb toward the summit of perfection . . .
Reginald Garrigou-Lagrange, *The Three Ages of the Spiritual Life*, trans. M. Timothea Doyle (St. Louis, Mo.: B. Herder, 1948), 2: 446.

He manifested his holiness in a great love of the Eucharist . . .
Foster, *The Life of Saint Thomas Aquinas*, 98.

Chapter 6

God has never wanted . . .
See Louis Chardon, *La Croce di Gesù*, trans. Giorgio Carbone (Bologna: Edizioni Studio Domenicano, 2004), 63. In English: *The Cross of Jesus*, Vol. 1, trans. Richard T. Murphy (St. Louis, Mo.: B. Herder, 1957).

Unrefined iron is . . .
This is an ancient image of divinization, drawn here from Matthias J. Scheeben, *The Glories of Divine Grace* (Rockford, Il.: TAN Books, 2000), 23. See ST II-II, q. 27, a. 7.

St. Catherine of Siena caught wind . . .
Bl. Raimondo da Capua, *S. Caterina da Siena: Legenda Maior*, trans. Giuseppe Tinagli (Siena: Edizioni Cantagalli, 1994), 149–50.

"give-away traits of the nonthinker"
Thomas Dubay, *Faith and Certitude* (San Francisco: Ignatius Press, 1985), 59.

John Paul II was surely correct when he said, "Driven . . ."
John Paul II, *Fides et Ratio: On the Relationship Between Faith and Reason* (1988), no. 4.

The ancient monk Evagrius . . .
Evagrius of Pontus, *The Greek Ascetic Corpus*, trans. Robert E. Sinkewicz (New York: Oxford University Press, 2013), especially the separate treatises: "On the Eight Thoughts," "The Monk: A Treatise on the Practical Life," and "On Thoughts." According to the ancient monk, the eight evil thoughts are gluttony, fornication, avarice, sadness, anger, acedia, and vainglory; pride caps them all.

In his *Disputed Questions on Evil* Thomas drew upon . . .
John Cassian's *Conferences* (the fifth addresses "eight principle vices") and Gregory the Great's *Moral Commentary on Job* offered a list that differs slightly from that of Evagrius: "envy" replaces "sadness," and "lust" replaces "fornication." See Aquinas, *On Evil*, trans. Richard Regan, ed. Brian Davies (New York: Oxford University Press, 2003), questions 8–15, plus question 16 "On Devils."

A number of modern authors have discussed them well . . .
See Rebecca Konyndyk DeYoung, *Glittering Vices: A New Look at the Seven Deadly Sins and Their Remedies*, 2nd ed. (Grand Rapids, MI: Brazos Press, 2020); Kevin Vost, *Seven Deadly Sins* (Manchester, NH: Sophia Institute Press, 2015); William Backus, *What Your Counselor Never Told You*, (Minneapolis, MN: Baker, 2000).

Instead, it may be useful to note a few other thoughts . . .
Inspiration for this chart comes, in part, from Thomas Brooks, *Precious Remedies against Satan's Devices* (Carlisle, PA: Banner of Truth Trust, 1968).

Personal causes for a polluted mind include . . .
Some of these are mentioned in Dubay, *Faith and Certitude*, 93–102.

Evagrius wisely notes that to overcome disordered passions . . .
Evagrius, "On Thoughts," in *The Greek Ascetic Corpus*, 154, 157.

Aquinas follows Augustine and explains that for every rational being . . .
For the following exposition, see his *Commentary on John*, c. 1, lect. 1.

As St. John of the Cross beautifully expressed . . .
The Ascent of Mount Carmel in *The Complete Works of John of the Cross*, trans. Kieran Kavanaugh and Otilio Rodriguez (Washington, DC: ICS Publications, 1991), II, 22.3.

Thomas notes that "a word from the mouth . . ."
Commentary on Ephesians, c. 4, lect. 9, n. 259.

Aquinas explains: those who speak evilly . . .
Commentary on Matthew, c. 12, lect. 2, n. 1039.

Not only pernicious, vile speech will be condemned—so will every single . . .
See Craig S. Keener, *The Gospel of Matthew: A Socio-Rhetorical Commentary* (Grand Rapids, MI: William B. Eerdmans, 2009), 367.

Accordingly, Sacred Scripture teaches . . .
Virtues and vices of the tongue receive much treatment in biblical wisdom literature. Among many, many examples, consider: "Let every man be quick to hear, slow to speak, slow to anger. . . . If any one thinks he is religious, and does not bridle his tongue but deceives his heart, this man's religion is vain" (Jas 1:19, 26; also 3:3–12). "Blessed is the man that does not blunder with his lips" (Sir 14:1). "Do not praise not a man before you hear him reason, for this is the test of men" (Sir 27:7).

. . . "wicked tongues," identified by St. Thomas of Villanova . . .
Sermon on the Fourth Sunday after Easter, quoted in entry "Lingua," in
Tobias Lohner, *Bibliotheca Manualis Concionatoria* (Paris: Hippolitum
Walzer, 1887), 715. He lists eleven; I added "the never-ending tongue"
and "the cursing tongue."

The ancient Jewish writer . . .
Philo, "On the Confusion of Tongues," in *The Works of Philo*, trans. C.
D. Yonge (Peabody, Mass.: Hendrickson, 1993), X (33-34), p. 237.

Saint Raymond Nonnatus . . .
See 31A: "Saint Raymond Nonnat, Cardinal," in Paul Guérin, *Les Petits
Bollandistes: Vies des Saints*, 7th ed., Vol. 10 (Paris: Bloud et Barral, 1865),
360.

Let us make the prayer of the Psalmist our own . . .
See also: "I said, 'I will guard my ways, that I may not sin with my
tongue'" (Ps 39:1). There is a blessing attached to being silent at the right
time: "What man is there who desires life, and covets many days, that he
may enjoy good? Keep your tongue from evil" (Ps 34:12–13).

In 1948, Pope Pius XII . . .
Radio Message to the U.S. National Catechetical Congress in Boston
(October 26, 1946). Quoted in John Paul II, *Reconciliatio et Paenitentia*
(Reconciliation and Penance), no. 18.

**Within the Church, John Paul II pointed out, "some are inclined .
. ."**
Reconciliatio et Paenitentia, no. 18.

Sin is a deliberate act . . .
See ST I-II, q. 21, a. 1; II-II, q. 163, a. 1.

**Focusing on the role of the will and its love, Augustine describes sin
. . .**
See *On the Free Choice of the Will*, I.16.35.

Augustine explains, "Sin is the will to retain . . ."
De duabus animabus, 11.15, quoted in James Wetzel, "Sin," in *Augustine through the Ages: An Encyclopedia*, ed. Allan D. Fitzgerald (Grand Rapids, MI: William B. Eerdmans, 1999), 801.

Following Aquinas, Pope John Paul II explained that "The morality of the human act . . ."
Veritatis Splendor, no. 78. The following quotations are from ibid., no. 78, no. 80 respectively. See ST I-II, q. 18, a. 2; and 19, a. 2: "The goodness of the will depends on only one thing, which per se makes it good in act, namely, the object, and not from circumstances, which are something like accidents of the act."

Aquinas recognizes that there are some acts "that have deformity . . ."
Quodlibet IX, q. 7, a. 2, co.

He explains, "a good intention is not enough . . ."
Collationes in decem praeceptis (Explanation of the Ten Commandments), a. 1, co.

They do not constitute the essence of the act . . .
See ST I-II, q. 7, a. 1.

John Paul II added: genocide . . .
Veritatis Splendor, no. 80, quoting *Gaudium et Spes*, 27.

In the seventeenth century, Pascal . . .
Blaise Pascal, *The Provincial Letters*, trans. A. J. Krailsheimer (New York: Penguin, 1967), Letter VII, p. 104.

Pascal's pointed pen illustrated what John Paul II insisted on . . .
The rest of this paragraph rephrases *Veritatis Splendor*, no. 82.

In addition to distinguishing sins . . .
These two ways of distinguishing sins do not correspond one-to-one: most mortal sins are intrinsically evil, but not all are. For example, purposely avoiding Sunday worship is a mortal sin but not intrinsically evil, because there might be mitigating circumstances, such as grave illness, that make the fulfillment of one's duty impossible. Similarly, lying is always wrong, but not all lies are mortal sins, because some might be evil

but of a very minor sort, such as a husband lying to his wife that clothes look nice on her.

Sin is a sort of "sickness of the soul" . . .
ST I-II, q. 88, a. 1.

In contrast, venial sins are not "unto death" . . .
ST I-II, q. 88, a. 1, ad 1. The Council of Trent infallibly declared that there is a difference between mortal sin: see Sess. 6., c. 11, "Men, however just and holy they may be, fall, sometimes at least, into those slight and daily sins that are also called venial, they do not on that account cease to be just" (DS 1537). And Can. 23, "If anyone says that a man once justified cannot sin again and cannot lose grace and that therefore the man who falls and sins was never truly justified; or, on the contrary, says that once justified can avoid all sins, even venial ones, throughout his entire life, unless it be by a special privilege of God as the Church holds of the Blessed Virgin, let him be anathema." John Paul II refers to these passages from Aquinas and Trent in *Reconciliatio et Paenitentia*, no. 17, adding in a solemn manner, "With the whole tradition of the church, we call mortal sin the act by which man freely and consciously rejects God, his law, the covenant of love that God offers, preferring to turn in on himself or to some created and finite reality, something contrary to the divine will (*conversio ad creaturam*). This can occur in a direct and formal way in the sins of idolatry, apostasy and atheism; or in an equivalent way as in every act of disobedience to God's commandments in a grave matter. Man perceives that this disobedience to God destroys the bond that unites him with his life principle: It is a mortal sin, that is, an act which gravely offends God and ends in turning against man himself with a dark and powerful force of destruction."

Augustine gives another comparison . . .
Letter 104, c. 4, no. 14 (PL 33:394).

Hence, St. Paul says . . .
See Lohner, "Lingua," 694. Also, ST I-II, q. 89, a. 2.

Aquinas argues that the objective nature of reality . . .
Commentary on the Apostle's Creed, a. 7, co.

One of the many visions of St. Brigid of Sweden . . .
The following exposition is from *The Revelations of St. Birgitta of Sweden Volume 2: Liber Caelestis, Books IV-V*, trans. Denis Searby (Oxford: Oxford University Press, 2008), 98–100.

A high level of virtue may be seen in the example of Jérôme Lejeune . . .
See, Clara Lejeune-Gaymard, *Life is a Blessing: A Biography of Jerome Lejeune: Geneticist, Doctor, Father*, trans. Michael J. Miller (San Francisco, CA: Ignatius Press, 2001). See also, CE Editors, "French Pro-Life Geneticist Jerome Lejeune to be Considered for Beatification," *Catholic Exchange*, 27 February 2004, https://catholicexchange.com/french-pro-life-geneticist-jerome-lejeune-to-be-considered-for-beatification.

Moral *incontinence* can be defined . . .
Commentary on Aristotle's Nicomachean Ethics, bk. VII, lect. 1, no. 1294.

A qualitative study found . . .
S. Power, S. Meaney, and K. O'Donoghue, "Fetal Medicine Specialist Experiences of Providing a New Service of Termination of Pregnancy for Fatal Fetal Anomaly: A Qualitative Study," *BJOG: An International Journal of Obstetrics and Gynaecology*, (September 15, 2020): 1-9, https://doi.org/10.1111/1471-0528.16502, at 5.

The result is that a person with vice . . .
Commentary on Aristotle's Nicomachean Ethics, bk. VII, lect. 3, no. 1336.

The deep-seated bad habits of vice encompass the whole person . . .
Commentary on Aristotle's Nicomachean Ethics, bk. VII, lect. 7, no. 1409.

Kermit Gosnell
Seth R. Williams, Report of the Grand Jury, Court of Common Pleas, First Judicial District of Pennsylvania (January 14, 2011). See also Samuel W. Calhoun, "Stopping Philadelphia Abortion Provider Kermit Gosnell and Preventing Others Like Him: An Outcome that Both Pro-Choicers and Pro-Lifers Should Support," *Villanova Law Review*, Vol. 57, no. 1 (2012): 1-43. "Fox 29 Speaks With Dr. Gosnell." WTXF-TV. 25, February, 2010, https://web.archive.org/web/20141118020955/http://www.myfoxphilly.com/story/17575375/fox-29-speaks-with-dr-gosnell.

Utilizing language that Aquinas would recognize, Norman Doidge explains . . .
See *The Brain that Changes Itself* (New York: Penguin, 2007). A warning is in order: chapter four contains extremely perverse case studies that readers should avoid.

Studies have shown that addictions to drugs such as cocaine, and habitual activities . . .
Doidge, *The Brain that Changes Itself*, 107. He cites Colleen A. McClung and Eric J. Nestler, "Neuroplasticity Mediated by Altered Gene Expression," *Neuropsychopharmacology: Official Publication of the American College of Neuropsychopharmacology* 33, no. 1 (January 2008): 3–17.

As one author has said, "Vice . . ."
Lohner, "Lingua," 693. He cites the work as S. Bernardus *ad Fratres de Monte Dei*, but it is now recognized that the work is by William of St. Thierry, a more accurate version of which is published as, Guillaume de Saint-Thierry, *Un Traité de la Vie Solitaire: Epistola ad Fratres de Monte-Dei*, ed. and trans. M.-M. Davy (Paris: Librairie Philosophique J. Vrin, 1940).

Aquinas illustrates: "the angry man . . ."
ST I-II, q. 72, a. 7, co.

Despair and presumption follow next . . .
ST I-II, q. 72, a. 7, ad 2.

Gregory the Great explains: "when the sin . . ."
Moralia in Iob, or Morals on the Book of Job, trans. James Bliss (Ex Fontibus, 2012), Book IV, c. 27, n. 51, p. 201.

As an emotion, despair is "the privation of hope . . ."
ST I-II, q. 40, a. 4, ad 3.

Sometimes when a sinner considers the reachability of God, he might despair . . .
ST II-II, q. 20, a. 1, ad 2.

Secondarily, despair is bound to hedonism within a vicious habit loop . . .
Aquinas uses the word *luxuria*, which often is translated as "lust," but this vice extends itself to other pleasures excessively as well. See ST II-II, q. 153, a. 1; *Disputed Questions on Evil*, q. 15, a. 1.

. . . then this disordered love "leads man . . ."
ST II-II, q. 20, a. 4.

But despair also causes hedonism, because "when hope is given up . . ."
ST II-II, q. 20, a. 3, co.

Others presume against the Holy Spirit . . .
See ST II-II, q. 21, a. 1.

It is a very grave sin . . .
ST II-II, q. 21, a. 1, ad 1.

Presumption also contradicts Christ . . .
This point is made by Aquinas in ibid., as well as John Bunyan in "The Jerusalem Sinner Saved: or, Good News for the Vilest of Men," in *The Works of John Bunyan* Vol. I (Carlisle, PA: Banner of Truth Trust, 1991; reprint of 1854 ed.), 93.

"I was wretched . . ."
Augustine, *Confessions*, trans. Frank J. Sheed (Indianapolis: Hackett, 1993), IV, cc. 6 and 7, pp. 55–56.

"Grant me chastity and continence, but not yet."
Confessions, VIII, c. 7, p. 139.

In the direction towards which I had turned my face . . .
Confessions, VIII, c. 11, pp. 144–45.

A child's voice said, *tolle, lege* . . .
Confessions, VIII, c. 12, p. 146.

Then God gave Augustine a greater grace, as he said to God, "By Your gift . . ."

Confessions, IX, c. 1, p. 151.

. . . his prayer became, "O Charity . . ."
Confessions, X, c. 29, p. 193. Translation slightly emended.

Chapter 7

St. Martin of Tours . . .
See 11 Novembre: "Saint Martin Évêque du Tours," in Paul Guérin, *Les Petits Bollandistes: Vies des Saints*, 7th ed., Vol. 13 (Paris: Bloud et Barral, 1865), 335-6. See also, *Sulpicius Severus: The Complete Works*, trans. Richard J. Goodrich (Mahwah, NJ: Paulist Press, 2016), 52–54.

Summarized in the chart . . .
See Aquinas, *Commentary on the Psalms*, 1, no. 2.

St. Robert Bellarmine interprets this . . .
Robert Bellarmine, *Explanatio in Psalmos* Vol. 2, ed. Augustino Crampon (Paris: Ludovicus Vives, 1861), 131.

Commenting on this passage . . .
Aquinas *Commentary on John*, c. 15, lect. 1, no. 1992.

Augustine adds a fifth . . .
See *In Evangelium Ioannis tractatus centum viginti quatuor*, tract. 86, no. 3 (PL 35: 1852).

Plutarch reports of Alexander the Great . . .
Lives, vol. 2, 142.

"charity is normally in perpetual growth"
Jean-Pierre Torrell, *Saint Thomas Aquinas: Spiritual Master* (Washington, D.C.: The Catholic University of America Press, 2003), 353.

**. . . as charity increases, it further augments one's capacity for increase
. . .**
ST II-II, q. 24, a. 7.

"transvaluation of values"
Nietzsche uses the term "Umwertung aller Werte," revaluation or transvaluation of all values as a rejection of the nineteenth-century corrupt
version of Christian values by which he was surrounded. See the end
of his work *Antichrist* in *The Portable Nietzsche*, ed. and trans. Walter
Kaufman (New York: Penguin Books, 1982), 656.

Sin corrupts all of our faculties . . .
ST I-II, q. 85, a. 3. I changed language for clarity: he says sin induces
weakness in the irascible appetite (which is perfected by fortitude), and
concupiscence in the concupiscible appetite.

St. Paul teaches, "the sensual man . . ."
Douay-Rheims translation of the Vulgate, which Aquinas used. The
RSV of 1 Cor 2:14 reads, "The unspiritual man does not receive the
gifts of the Spirit of God, for they are folly to him, and he is not able to
understand them because they are spiritually discerned."

**Commenting on this passage Aquinas explains that a person is called
"sensual" . . .**
Commentary on I Corinthians, c. 2, lect. 3, n. 112.

. . . as Aristotle said, "as a person is . . ."
That is Aquinas's more succinct phrase. Aristotle says them same in different ways: "the sort of person each of us is, whatever that may be,
determines how the end, too, appears to him," in *Nicomachean Ethics*,
trans. Sarah Broadie and Christopher Rowe (Oxford: Oxford University
Press, 2002), III.5, 1114b1-2. Also, "each type [of person], if he is not
acting for some further end, speaks and acts in the way corresponding to
his nature, and lives his life in that way."

**Wallowing in the mud of the world, the piggish person is unable to
look at the stars without dirt in his eyes: "a man given to sense . . ."**
Aquinas, *Commentary on I Corinthians*, c. 2, lect. 3, n. 114.

Many of his sermons sound this theme: "Religion is in itself . . ."
I will cite Newman's *Parochial and Plain Sermons* according to the volume, sermon, and page numbers of the eight volume series (London: Longmans, Green & Co, 1907), e.g., *PPS* I, 1: 1. All italics are in the original unless otherwise noted. The entire series can be found online at http://www.newmanreader.org/works. *PPS* I, 2:24.

Newman says about religion . . .
The remaining quotations in this paragraph are from *PPS*, VII, 2:17, 18-19, 21-22; and VII, 14:196, respectively.

John of the Cross writes, "By the very fact . . ."
The Ascent of Mt. Carmel, III.19.3.

He quotes the book of Wisdom . . .
John of the Cross seems to quote an alternate version of the Vulgate, or his own translation thereof. The RSV of Wis 4:12 reads, "For the fascination of wickedness obscures what is good, and roving desire perverts the innocent mind."

The consequences of this state are "many kinds of serious harm" . . .
Ascent, III.19.5. The following quotations are from ibid., 6, and 7, respectively.

As Aquinas said, "whatever a person assigns to himself . . ."
Commentary on II Corinthians, c. 4, n. 124.

Even worse are the wicked who . . .
The following quotations in the paragraph are from John of the Cross, *Ascent*, III.19.9 and 10.

St. John Henry Newman sharply observed . . .
PPS I, 1:7-8.

Drawing upon his own experience, Aquinas argues . . .
ST I-II, q. 31, a. 5.

John of the Cross similarly attested . . .
Ascent, III.20.2.

As Newman said, "The pleasures of sin . . ."
PPS VII, 14:197.

. . . as John Paul II points out . . .
General Audience 22 July 1987, in *A Catechesis on the Creed, Volume II: Jesus: Son and Savior* (Boston: Pauline Books and Media, 1996), 181.

Accordingly, Christ prayed that his disciples . . .
ST III, q. 21, a. 1.

A Carmelite spiritual writer put it this way . . .
Gabriel of St. Mary Magdalene, *Divine Intimacy: Meditations on the Interior Life for Every Day of the Year*, trans. Discalced Carmelites Nuns of Boston (New York: Desclée, 1963), 172.

Augustine showed that such prayer is possible . . .
Ennaraciones sobre los Salmos [Expositions on the Psalms], Vol. III, ed. Balbino Martin Perez (Madrid: Biblioteca de Autores Cristianos, 1966), 85.1, p. 216. The edition is dual-language Spanish and Latin. My translation.

Prayer can be defined . . .
ST II-II, q. 83, a. 1, ad 2: "The will moves the reason to its end: wherefore nothing hinders the act of reason, under the motion of the will, from tending to an end such as charity which is union with God. Now prayer tends to God through being moved by the will of charity . . . in the same sense Damascene says (*De Fide Orth.* iii, 24) that 'prayer is the raising up of the mind to God.'"

According to Aquinas, authentic prayer must be . . .
This is a synthesis of the various lists in: *Commentary on the Gospel of John*, 16, lect. 6, no. 2142; *Exposition on the Lord's Prayer*, prol.; ST II-II, q. 83.

Aquinas clarifies that Christ's promise here . . .
ST II-II, q. 83, a. 15, ad 2.

Because Christ wants to have us join him . . .
St. Paul echoes: "Pray at all times in the Spirit" (Eph 6:18); "Continue steadfastly in prayer" (Col 4:2); "pray constantly" (1 Th 5:17).

In the words of St. Alphonsus Liguori . . .
Hence, his book, *The Great Means of Salvation*, trans. Eugene Grimm
(Brooklyn: Redemptorist Fathers, 1927), 19.

"activism" and "Quietism"
See the brief discussion in Chapter Five.

"ultra-supernaturalism"
Ronald Knox uses the term in a slightly different way, as referring to
unreasonable expectations of miracles—which is clearly related to unreasonable expectations of grace in general, in my meaning. See *Enthusi-
asm: A Chapter in the History of Religion* (Notre Dame, IN: University of
Notre Dame Press, 1950), 2, 1l.

Nevertheless, quietism has been condemned by the Church . . .
See, for example, the Church's teaching: "But all, contemplatives as well
as those practicing meditation, should know that they are in no way
exempt from the external duties of religion and piety that are wont to be
practiced by the faithful in the Catholic Church, such as the use of sacraments and sacramentals, the visitation of churches and the observance of
fasts, the listening to sermons, and the other works of spiritual corporal
mercy; on the contrary, it would be a great scandal to the faithful if,
under the pretext of contemplation meditation, any of the aforesaid pre-
cepts were neglected by them," in "Draft for the Instruction of the Holy
Office Drawn up by Cardinal Girolamo Casanate, ca. October 1682,"
no. 11, Heinrich Denzinger, *Enchiridion symbolorum*, 43rd edition, ed.
Peter Hünermann (San Francisco: Ignatius Press, 2010), 2191. Also, the
condemnations of the errors of Miguel de Molinos, Denzinger-Hüner-
mann nos. 2201-2269 passim.

Hence, Aquinas says, a supernatural effect . . .
SCG III, c. 70, no. 8.

In Aquinas's words, "After baptism . . ."
ST III, q. 39, a. 5.

Liguori builds upon this: "without the divine assistance . . ."
The Great Means of Salvation, 26, 27.

"the tool of tools"
De Anima, 432a1.

St. Alphonsus's beautiful teaching: "I am certain that by prayer . . ."
Liguori, *The Great Means of Salvation*, 233.

St. Thérèse of Lisieux . . .
Story of A Soul, 258.

Hence, another spiritual writer aptly states, "prayer is to the spiritual life . . ."
Alphonsus Rodriguez, *The Practice of Christian and Religious Perfection* Vol. I (Dublin: James Duffy and Sons, 1882), 236–37.

He notes that one can "pray continually" . . .
See ST II-II, q. 83, a. 14, ad 2 and 4.

St. Simeon the New Theologian . . .
"Three Methods of Attention and Prayer," in *Writings from the Philokalia on Prayer of the Heart*, trans. K. Kadloubovsky and G. E. H. Palmer (London: Faber and Faber, 1951), 156–57.

St. Bonaventure tells the tale of St. Dominic . . .
Dante Alighieri, *The Paradiso*, trans. Robert Hollander and Jean Hollander (New York: Anchor, 2007), XII.55–56, 66, 70–71, 142–44.

. . . the good of grace in the soul is greater than the natural good of the whole universe . . .
ST I-II, q. 113, a. 9, ad 2

. . . perfection does not consist in some exterior act but rather in following Christ, which is done through charity.
Commentary on Matthew, c. 22, lect. 2, no. 373

Let us suppose that a person has a candle . . .
Commentary on Colossians, c. 2, lect. 1, no. 82.

Those who knew him attested . . .
Foster, *The Life of Saint Thomas Aquinas*, 37 and 98.

. . . the highest form of prayer an activity of all the greatest habits together.

"Here, in this culminating point of prayer, the fruit of the theological virtues, the knowledge of faith, the love of hope, and that of charity tend, under the influence of the Holy Ghost, to fuse in a gaze of faithful and generous love, which is the beginning of contemplation: Christian contemplation which bears on God and the humanity of Christ. . . . This prayer begins to penetrate and to taste the mysteries of salvation: the nature of the indwelling of the Blessed Trinity in our souls, the mystical body of Christ, and the communion of the saints. Gradually it introduces us into the intimacy of Christ, the intimacy of love." Garrigou-Lagrange, *The Three Ages of the Spiritual Life*, 1:450-51.